CLASSICAL TAMIL
LOVE POETRY

CLASSICAL TAMIL LOVE POETRY

Ainkurunuru or Five Hundred Short Poems

M NAZIR ALI

PARTRIDGE

A Penguin Random House Company

To order additional copies of this book, contact
Partridge India
000 800 10062 62
www.partridgepublishing.com/india
orders.india@partridgepublishing.com

CONTENTS

PART I: MARUTAM ORAMPOKIAR

PART II: NEIDAL AMMUVANAR

PART III: KURINJI KAPILAR

PART IV: PALAI ODALANDAYAR

PART V: MULLAI PEYANAR

ACKNOWLEDGMENTS

I acknowledge with gratitude the inspiration and encouragement provided by M.L. Thangappa, teacher, poet and translator and two times winner of the *Sahitya Akademi* award.

Dr P. Raja, a bilingual writer of repute and the editor of *Transfire*, a bimonthly devoted to translation, ran his pen over my manuscript and came up with suggestions which I was delighted to carry out.

Dr T. Selvam, Associate Professor of Tamil, Tagore Arts College, with his years of experience in guiding research in Sangam literature, helped in bringing clarity to some of the subtler concepts governing the akam conventions.

Mr. John Sudhakar, friend and colleague, looking at the translation with the eye of a connoisseur, helped me in ironing out the discrepancies.

I thank my students to whom I taught "National Literature in Translation," and whose enthusiasm provided the germ of the idea for this translation.

M. Nazir Ali

FOREWORD

M. L. Thangappa

Ainkurunuru is a fine piece of work from the Sangam classics. Written in the direct, lucid style typical of the Sangam classics, it still has a charm of its own which I suppose is due to its terseness and brevity. Each poem consists of not more than five lines. The poems are well-knit and so carefully written that not even a single word can be pointed out as superfluous.

It is good that Nazir Ali has chosen this beautiful work for translation and brought out a complete rendering of it in modern, lucid, readable English.

I need not here tell you what *Ainkurunuru* is about, for Nazir being the editor himself has given us a very good introduction to his work which tells us in brief about Sangam literature in general and about *Ainkurunuru* in particular. He has briefly summed up the five tinais and has supplied the examples which capture the basic ingredients of each tinai.

In Tamil Akam poetry the lover and his ladylove are called *Thalaivan* and *Thalaivi*. Translators have translated these words in different ways, but Nazir has chosen to retain the Tamil epithets without translating them into English. He has also not felt it necessary to furnish the elaborate tinai descriptions of the poems. The heading itself tells us what the poem is about.

Much has been said about the art of translation and a lot of rules are laid down to make a good translation. Many people go by these rules and do well. But as far as the translation of poetry is concerned, it is the evoking of the poetic feeling that is more important than the rest of the rules. Nazir has the poetic turn of mind with which he has absorbed the spirit and feel of the original poems and brought them into his translations.

That is why the translations are lively, charming and beautiful.

It is no exaggeration to say that I was swept off my feet the moment I started reading this wonderful work. It is such a superb English rendering ever made of a work from the Sangam classics; delightful to read and delightful to think of.

Nazir Ali is not a translator. He is a poet who has brought out the poetry of *Ainkurunuru*.

When someone who has not read the original comes in contact with a translation, they may go about examining the merits and demerits of the work as a translation. And people who know the original start comparing the translation with the original. I must say—to the credit of Nazir—that my experience was different. When I started reading Nazir's work for the first time I was not conscious for a few seconds that I was reading an English translation of *Ainkurunuru*. I felt I was reading the original itself! Becoming conscious of the translation a few seconds later I was delightfully surprised at the skill with which Nazir has brought about a faithful translation.

I must frankly admit here that I am no scholarly judge of translations. Having taken to translation as a hobby, I haven't cared much about the form and structure and the craftsmanship involved in translation. Even as I judge poetry by the delight or pleasure it gives me, I judge a translation by the pleasure it gives me. Other things come later.

So, let me not try to enumerate here the several merits of this translation, which it amply has, but simply draw attention to some of the striking phrases and expressions which Nazir has employed and which make the work beautiful.

Here are a few passages taken at random in which the simplicity of the original is expressed with the same simplicity in English:

In my chief's land
the mango blooms
and small, smelly fish abound
in the cool water spots. (10)

When evening comes
the blue flower
in the dark blue backwater closes. (116)

The winged bug,
which has six tiny legs,
lays eggs on the lotus
with a hundred petals.
The tall, bamboo-like reed,
hollow inside,
swaying in the wind,
destroys them. (20)

The deep feelings of the lovers are brought out in a manner that touches our heart.

He has not come
but the season has come

for the neem tree
to shed its bright flowers
and for him to whisper
sweet nothings
to bring me around. (350)

My stout heart refuses
to accompany me.

It wants to go back
to my wife
I've left behind.
She must be thinner now,
the armlets she wears
slipping down. (329)

Friend, live long. Listen.
The tiny-leaved gooseberry
grows closely.
My poor, devoted heart
follows my lover through
the sun-burnt stones.
My kohled eyes,
like blue flowers,
keep crying. (334)

Descriptions which are subtle and have a hidden meaning
pose no difficulties for Nazir.

Friend, the sweet-smelling
tender mangoes fall down,
their stems broken,
from the scarred mango tree
like falling hailstones
and tribes living in dry lands
string them up. (213)

The hillmen burn sandalwood
whose smoke mixes
with the smell of honey
in the mountains.

If the chief of this hill country
marries me,
will my mother
too approve of it? (253)

The flame-coloured tiger roars.
Frightened,
the male monkey
bounds up the mountaintop.

The chief of the mountains
went away leaving me alone.
While going,
he carried away
the beauty of my arms
and my sleep. (274)

Ainkurunuru has given us beautiful vignettes of family life for
which there is no compare in all of Sangam literature. Nazir has
rendered them with the same beauty in English.

Like a fawn
that lies
between the stag and its mate,
their son sleeps between them.

Such bliss like this
is rarely found
on this earth
covered by the vast blue sky. (401)

The mother hugs
her baby son.
The father hugs
her from behind
with desire.

This is a scene sweet
as the music
of the bard's harp.
It shows their goodness too. (402)

And here are a few more which gave me great delight:

The wild boar,
its curved tusks
like the crescent moon,
makes love to its mate
dark as Indian currant. (264)

The huge branch
of the tiger claw tree,
bearing sweet-smelling flowers,
is drenched
by pounding waves. (150)

The elegant stork
that went to console
the grieving white crane
over the death of its fledgling
roams with its mate
in the groves
of the vast beautiful shore. (158)

Driven by a desire
to make wealth,
I left you.
The path through the mountains
was long and tedious.

When I returned
by the same path
spurred by your bejewelled beauty,
it was surprisingly short. (359)

It is regrettable that there is not much exchange of thoughts
and very little interaction between the Tamil and English
teachers of our universities. There are also not that many
attempts at translation from one language to the other. Nazir
is one among a few who are disposed otherwise, who have
come to love their language in spite of their English connection.

His translation shows how deeply he has studied *Ainkurunuru* and how intimately came to have a poet's rapport with it.

It is a good and welcome sign that Nazir has taken upon himself the mighty task of translating all the five hundred poems from one of the most beautiful works from the Sangam classics.

INTRODUCTION

The Age

When it comes to a discussion of Sangam Age, it is easy enough to become bogged down by questions like 1) Was there a Sangam or an academy of learned men who legislated on matters related to language and poetics? 2) If there was a Sangam then how long it lasted and 3) Whether there was one or three Sangams as claimed. Claims range from texts that assert that three Sangams existed spanning over a period of 10, 000 years (*Iraiyanar Akapporul* 5-6) to sceptical critics who consider that Sangam is a fabrication (Hart: 9-10). And there are poets like A. K. Ramanujan who maintain that Sangam is not so much a community or fraternity of poets but a set of consensual poetic practices of five or six generation of poets (251). Where facts are shrouded in a fog of myth and myth-making in which gods reputedly rubbed shoulders with mortals in poetic compositions and competitions and when many poets existed bearing the same name, it is better to exercise caution and stick to facts, which, by common consent, are acknowledged to be facts.

The Sangam Age or what Kamil Zvelebil calls the "bardic" phase lasted from 150 BCE to ca. 250 CE. This corresponds to the time when almost all the extant Sangam Classics were being produced. This was followed by the Post Classical period when most of the *Pathinen Kizh Kanakku* texts were produced and which lasted from ca. 250 CE to 600 CE (*Companion.* 17). Based on the archaeological excavations at Adichanallur, near Tirunelveli, Zvelebil draws the following conclusions:

1.   The people were "militaristic" and the use of iron and horses made them practically invincible.
2.   They worshipped Korravai, the goddess of victory, after a win in the battle.
3.   Their earliest poetry idealizes heroism in war and sacred rites were performed on instruments of war, including war drums.
4.   Their god of worship was Murugan and the small spears found in the site attest to this.
5.   They cultivated rice. (20-21)

Though these findings refer to the life of people who lived in the Pre-Sangam period, we find that these practices were still current in the Sangam Age too and neatly dovetail with the evidentiary material available in plenty in the Sangam texts. In the Sangam period there is a consolidation of impulses towards urbanization (the appearance of capitals like Madurai and port towns like Poompukar, Thondi, Korkai), a transition from the oral to the literate levels, growth of indigenous religions and the emergence of Tamil nationhood under the three kings and a greater level of prosperity affording leisure for cultural, artistic and sculptural activities. The number of Roman coins of the emperors of first and second centuries gives proof of a flourishing trade with the *Yavanas* or westerners.

The Texts

The Sangam Classics are divided into *Ettutokai* (The Eight Anthologies) and *Pattupattu* (The Ten Songs). *Tolkappiyam*, a text on grammar and linguistic analysis, is also an indivisible part of the Sangam Classics.

Ainkurunuru, Kuruntokai, Narrinai, Akananuru, Kalitokai, Pathirrupathu, Paripatal and *Purananuru* make the corpus of the *Ettuthokai*.

Pattupattu consists of *Thirumurugarruppadai* (also known as *Pulavar Arruppadai*), *Porunar Arruppadai, Sirupan Arruppadai, Perumpan Arruppadai, Mullai Pattu, Madurai Kanchi, Nedunalvadai, Kurinji Pattu, Pattinappalai and Malaipadukadam (*also known *as Kuthar Arruppadai).*

Pattupattu and the *Ettutokai* are together known as *Pathinen Mel Kanakku* or The Higher Eighteen.

The Post-Sangam Classics are classified as *Pathinen Kizh Kanakku* or The Lower Eighteen, among which the *Tirukkural* is the most significant.

Ainkurunuru as Akam Poetry

Cutting across the two corpuses of poems, namely *Ettuthokai* and *Pattupattu* with a total of 2,381 poems composed by 473 poets, we have two broad generic divisions known as Akam and Puram which may be roughly equated with subjective and objective poetry respectively. In actual practice, however, Akam is concerned with "all the phases of love between man and woman" and Puram contains "poems of war, of king's praise, of suppliants' requests, of mourning, of ethics" (Hart: 7). Out of this total of 2,381, the poems devoted to Akam alone amount to a massive 1862 sung by a vastly superior number of 378 poets. It would be better for a lay reader to understand some of the important conventions that govern Akam poetry as the five hundred short poems of *Ainkurunuru* are Akam poetry through and through. In this regard Kamil Zvelebil's *Literary Conventions in Akam Poetry* and Sp. Manickam's *Tamil Concept of Love in Ahattinai* are extremely useful reference texts.

Akam is divided into five major tinais or physiographical regions: kurinji, mullai, marutam, neidal and palai. Collectively they are known as *aintinai* or five tinais. A poem is composed against the backdrop of one of these tinais and it illustrates a specific mood or sentiment in a given time and season. The poems have a speaker and a listener and sometimes words are spoken deliberately loudly with a telling effect to be heard by a distant or hidden listener. Each tinai is considered appropriate for the conduct of a particular course of love like premarital (kalavu) or post marital love (karpu). Palai is the exception where both courses run concurrently. Besides briefly summing up each tinai, I shall also supply an example from *Ainkurunuru* which captures the basic ingredients of each tinai.

Kurinji: Mountain and the adjoining slopes in the cool season and clandestine meeting of the lovers prior to their marriage (*kalavu*):

Thozhi to thalaivi:

Mother, live long. Listen.
Will drought
affect your field of millet?
Look there.
His tall blue mountain
topped by rain clouds
looks like meat
covered in fat. (207)

This poem by Kapilar tells us of the apprehension of the thalaivi and how her thozhi consoles her. The thalaivi has been meeting the thalaivan secretly in the millet field but prolonged drought has withered the plants. Her parents may recall her from guarding millet and prevent her from meeting her lover. The thozhi points at the cloud-capped distant mountains of thalaivan using the striking simile of a cut of meat covered in fat. And what the thozhi says is of as much importance as what she does not say. She leaves the matter for the thalaivi to figure things out for herself. The poem functions in the same way that the thozhi does. It tells the reader to deduce that the distant rain clouds and the thalaivi's expectations are inter-related and the human world and the world of nature co-exist seamlessly. The thalaivan's mountains are experiencing rainfall relieving summer's heat. It is not only a good omen but contains the implied message that the thalaivan shall bring similar alleviation to thalaivi's suffering. And the simile that the thozhi has chosen to convey whets the appetite further. It is this refusal to pontificate that makes Akam poetry contemporary. The vocative 'Mother' that the thozhi uses refers indifferently to mother, foster mother, thalaivi and thozhi.

Mullai: Forest and the region close to it during the rainy season when the thalaivi awaits the return of thalaivan after their marriage (*karpu*):

Thalaivan to himself (within the hearing of thalaivi):

The monsoon mated
with the forest.
The forest grew festive.
My lady's beauty returned
with my own homecoming.
The fresh flowers
worn on her hair
drew a swarm of bees to them
as she made love to me.

It will be found that all the objects are paired to give a sense of union which is what mullai tinai is about: the monsoon and the forest, the bees and the flowers and finally, the two lovers. This is a poem of Peyanar.

Marutam: The farms and fields fed by the river in no specific season. The thalaivan's visits to the mistresses give the thalaivi a lot of heartburn. Male infidelity may be said to be the chief subject matter of marutam which occurs in the post-marital stage (karpu):

Thalaivi to the friends
of thalaivan refusing entry:

The purslane creeper
close to the house grew
long enough to entwine the reed.

My chief, whose land
is rich in water, is good, I say.
But my soft shoulders,
grown thinner
by his desertion, tell, 'No, he isn't.' (11)

In this poem of Orampokiar, the thalaivi tries desperately to hide her frustration and sorrow caused by the conduct of the thalaivan but the emaciation of her body betrays her true feelings. The purslane creeper grows long enough to slip out of the house and reach the reed just as the thalaivan's sexual adventures take him out of the bounds of domesticity. Unconvinced by the pledges of love from the thalaivan, the thalaivi rejects his overtures.

Neidal: The seashore in no particular season and the theme is about the secret meetings of the lovers and other such erotic matters prior to marriage (*kalavu*). If these meetings took place in day time, they were designated as *pagar kuri* and in the night, *iravuk kuri*:

Thalaivi to thozhi:

Long live, friend.
Yesterday the village called me
'the woman' of the chief
in whose country

tall waves smash
the white sand.

On hearing it
my mother asked me, 'Are you?'
Softly I replied, 'It's me!' (113)

The secret meetings of the lovers give room to gossip among
the womenfolk of the village (*alarvai pendir*, the compulsive
women gossipers) who call the thalaivi 'the woman of the
chief.' She is secretly pleased about being known such but
she is not in a position to admit it to her mother. That is why
she replies in an undertone, 'It's me!'. The tall waves crashing
is not mere nature description. It may imply the gossip mills
being active spreading stories. As A.K. Ramanujan says, 'Mere
nature or imagism in poetry would be uninteresting to classical
Tamil poets and critics, for it would not "signify"; it would be
a signifier without a signified, a landscape (*mutal* and *karu*)
without an *uri*, an appropriate human mood." (243) The subtle
play of feelings is brought out by this poem composed by
Ammuvanar.

Palai: During the harsh Tamil summers, vast tracts of forests
and mountains have a skeletal look and this is the region of
palai. Fittingly, the feelings described are sorrow induced by
separation as the lover goes out in search of wealth or goes
on war. This phase can be found in both pre and post marital
stages (*kalavu* and *karpu*):

Thozhi to thalaivan:

Chief on whose hilltops
clouds crawl,
those who walk in the hot sun
drape their heads
with the immaculate flowers
of the silk cotton tree.

Before you cross
that mountain there,
her grief would've grown
to a huge extent. (301)

In this poem by Odalandayar the thozhi tries to dissuade the
thalaivan from going on his hazardous journey to earn wealth
citing her friend's sorrow but only rarely succeeds in stopping
the thalaivan. The leafless cotton tree, the scorching sun, the
lonely traveller and the mood of intense sorrow coalesce with
each other so well that one becomes the index of the other.

Each tinai has its own animals, birds, plants, trees and flowers
and in the hands of the skilful poet all these natural elements
are seamlessly assimilated into the human world. And as
Prof. Manickam says, "The supreme test of the greatness of
an Akam poet lies in his minute knowledge of Nature and in
his power of artistically and appropriately handling Nature for
the embellishment of Akam elements" (205). Endorsing this
view, Varadarajan says that "These ancient poets do not treat
of Nature alone, but resort to it always to describe human
life in its varying aspects, chiefly love and war" (2). George
Hart observes in *The Poems of Ancient Tamil* "the complex
technique of suggestion" (161) used by these poems to make
their point.

Akam poetry is impersonal in the sense there is a convention
of "not naming" at work throughout the body of the poems.
The actors are identified on the basis of their region (*uran,
turaivan*) or by their profession (*uzhavan, uzhatti*) or by their
gender (*nampi, sirumi*).

The way an Akam poem succeeds in its task of communication
is through the deployment of *mutal, karu* and *uri*. Mutal which
means 'first' or 'the basic' makes the statement of place and
time. Karu identifies the flora and fauna of the region or the
people who inhabit it. These two give a local habitation and
a name lending what Henry James would call "the solidity of
specification." But the ancient Tamil poets do much more than

that. They use the mutal and karu in order to bring out the uri
which is actually the meat of the poem: the human feeling.
All these three orchestrate the meaning, not didactically but
through a subtle interplay of images, metaphors and similes.

The colophon attributes the job of compiling the poems of
Ainkurunuru to Pulaturai Murriya Kudalur Kizhar and the
poem attributed to him in *Purananuru* (229) commemorates
his patron and the Chera King Yanaikat Chey Mantarancheral
Irumporai who is credited with being instrumental in
commissioning this project.

Believed to have lived in 4 CE, Perunthevanar has composed
the invocations for *Ainkurunuru, Narrinai, Kuruntokai,
Akananuru* and *Purananuru* making scholars believe that they
are subsequent insertions. His invocation for *Ainkurunuru*
praises Lord Siva as the originator of the Underworld, the Earth
and the Heaven and who generously gives half of his body to
his Divine Consort:

All the three worlds appeared in order
under the shadow of his two divine feet
who gave half of his body
to his blue-bodied, pure-jewelled wife

Perunthevanar is also reputed to be the one who translated
The Mahabaratham besides contributing a poem apiece to
Akananuru and *Narrinai*.

A NOTE ON MY TRANSLATION

What drew me to Sangam literature is M. L. Thangappa's *Love Stands Alone: Selections from Tamil Sangam Poetry*. It is done in lucid, utterly idiomatic English and Sangam poetry, with its archaic language and plethora of qualifiers, suddenly took on a contemporary look and it came as a revelation to me. And once the language is modernized the sentiments and thoughts took on a kind of poignancy which I never thought I would find in poetry written a couple of millennia ago. There is no turning back since then. I read with avidity the translations of A. K. Ramanujan, George Hart and Martha Ann Selby and each one appealed to me for a variety of reasons. A.K. Ramanujan, being heir to Tamil and Kannada literatures is something of an insider and his years of teaching and training in Dravidian languages, besides being a foremost practising poet, have honed his skills as a translator. But I entertain the feeling that in translating the Tamil poems of the past, he has tilted the scales favouring the Western aesthetic perhaps in order to make them amenable to Western sensibilities. George Hart impresses me a lot with his scholarship and a little less with his art of translation. I am much indebted to his findings in *The Poems of Ancient Tamil*. Martha Ann Selby's translation is much better, though a little more lyricism will not hurt her renderings. She sees the individual trees very well but often misses the woods. Her translation is most faithful to the paraphrasable content of the poems but as poems they do not always succeed.

In order to individuate each poem, I have given a title, a feature not to be found in the mother text. And where the mutal and karu seem to have little or no bearing on the uri, I have given a brief explanation in the Notes coming at the end. If English and botanical names to plants and flowers are found to be too cumbersome, I have used their Tamil names and provided the English equivalents in the Notes. Diacritical marks have been avoided and spelling corresponds to the way the names are normally spoken in Tamil. I retained *thalaivan*, *thalaivi* and *thozhi* from the source text for the unmistakable cultural and semantic burden they carried much in the same way the Japanese terms *samurai* or *geisha* do.

THE TEXT OF AINKURUNURU

The first print edition of *Ainkurunuru* was brought out by Dr U. Ve. Swaminatha Iyyer in 1903 along with the old notes written by an anonymous commentator. These notes have attained the status of a minor classic quite disproportionate to their brevity. The service rendered by Dr Iyyer to Tamil studies cannot be underestimated as he has been instrumental in unearthing and publishing no less than five Sangam texts: *Pattupattu* (1889), *Purananuru*(1894), *Ainkurunuru* (1903), *Pathirrupathu* (1904) and *Paripatal* (1918).

I have used the Murray Rajam edition of 1957 for all textual references.

THE ACTORS

Thalaivi: The lady (who could be the wife as well as the ladylove)

Thalaivan: The chief (who could be the husband or lover or the chieftain of a particular landscape)

Thozhi: The girlfriend (the friend, guide and confidant of the lady)

The mistress

The foster mother of the lady

The mother of the lady

The bard (a musician, singer as well as messenger of the chief)

The priest

Travellers, messengers, a few brahmin priests and neighbours

The fish, fowl and beasts, plants and flowers of a given landscape

PART I

MARUTAM ORAMPOKIAR

Composed against a backdrop of fertile fields fed by rivers, Marutam has as its primary theme male infidelity and the consequent sorrow felt by the woman. The thozhi plays a significant role, counselling the thalaivan to give up his errant ways. She is sharp of tongue, resourceful and never misses an opportunity in reminding the thalaivan of the vastly nobler nature of the thalaivi in contrast to the mistress with whom he spends his time. The mango tree is prominent among the flora, the buffalo and the peacock among the fauna.

A total of one hundred and ten Sangam poems are attributed to Orampokiar. Apart from the hundred *Ainkurunuru* poems, he has composed two each for *Narrinai* and *Akananuru*, five for *Kuruntokai* and one for *Purananuru*. With the exception of two poems in *Kuruntokai*, all others belong to the tinai of marutam making him "the bard of marutam." He is the first poet to refer to the Festival of *Indra* (62) and the virgins fasting in the month of *Thai* (84) and the conquered soldiers made to eat grass (4).

1. The wish list

In reply to the thalaivan's query as to what thoughts passed through their minds during the period he left them, the thozhi replies on behalf of the thalaivi and herself.

1. May you live long

'Long live Athan and Avini.
Let there be a plenitude
of paddy and gold!'
so wished my lady.

For my part I wished,
'Let my chief whose town
brings in new wealth
with portia breaking into bud
and in whose waters
small fish breed,
live long.
Let his bard too live long.'

2. Love her forever

'Long live Athan and Avini.
Let the farm yield more,
let the poor seek us,'
so wished my lady.

For my part I wished,
'The pale water lily
vies with the many-petalled blue lily
in my chief's land of cool lakes.
May he love my lady
in all ages to come.'

3. Happy married life

'Long live Athan and Avini.
Let milk flow.
Let the buffaloes grow in number,'
so wished my lady.

For my part I wished,
'May peasants return home
with plenty of paddy
after planting the seeds.
Let the marital life
of the chief of flower
country brighten.'

4. No common ground

'Long live Athan and Avini.
Let his enemies eat grass.
Let the priests
recite their prayers,'
so wished my lady.

For my part I wished,
'My chief in whose lands
sugarcane blooms and paddy dries
shouldn't let his chest
become common ground.'

5. Park on our porch

'Long live Athan and Avini.
Let there be no hunger.
Let all ailments leave us for good,'
so wished my lady.

For my part I wished,
'In my chief's land
the crocodile eats the big fish
living in the same pond.
Let my chief's chariot
stay parked only on our porch.'

6. Marry her at once

'Long live Athan and Avini.
Let my king's anger lessen.
Let his reign extend
for many years,'
so wished my lady.

For my part I wished,
'Let my chief
in whose cool ponds
lotuses bloom marry her.
Let my father
too consent to this.'

7. Take my lady

'Long live Athan and Avini.
May virtues grow
and vices end,'
so wished my lady.

For my part I wished,
'In my chief's land
storks build their nests
on the branches of *marutam*
growing near cool ponds.
Let him take
my lady to his place.'

8. Keep your vows

'Long live Athan and Avini.
Let there be a just rule.
Let all theft come to an end,'
so wished my lady.

For my part I wished,
'Peacocks shelter
in the swaying branches
of the mango tree.
Let my chief keep all his vows.'

9. Grounds for calumny

'Long live Athan and Avini.
May all good things grow.
Let evil come to an end,'
so wished my lady.

For my part I wished,
'The stork eats fish
and finds shelter
in the haystack in my chief's land.
Let not their love
become a reason for calumny.'

10. Take her home

'Long live Athan and Avini.
Let there be rain.
And all wealth grow,'
so wished my lady.

For my part I wished,
'In my chief's land
the mango blooms

and small, smelly fish abound
in the cool water spots.
Let him take
my lady to his place.'

2. The reed

11. The language of the shoulders

Thalaivi to the friends of thalaivan:

The purslane creeper
close to the house grew
long enough to entwine the reed.

My chief, whose land
is rich in water, is good, I say.
But my soft shoulders,
grown thinner
by his desertion, tell, 'No, he isn't.'

12. The body doesn't lie

Thalaivi to herself:

The blooms of the reed
look to be the same
as those of sugarcane.

Even if I bear
the rejection of my chief,
alas! my soft shoulders sag.

13. Working women

Thalaivi to the friends
of thalaivan refusing entry:

Like the handsome bristles
which adorn the horse's head
the reed blooms
on the river bank!

Even when the village sleeps,
his women around him
are ignorant of it.

14. Sleep

Thalaivi to thozhi:

In my chieftain's land
the reed nudges
the tender leaves
of the scarred mango tree.

When I bury my face
on his broad chest
it gives me
such delightful sleep.

15. A stranger

Thalaivi to thozhi:

My chieftain is a lover
to the women
bathing in the sand-banked river
wearing bright leaves.

Though he is of this old town
where reed grows,
he has also grown alien to it.

16. No entry

Thozhi to the friends
of thalaivan refusing entry:

Long-stemmed flowers
bloom on the reed
which is hollow inside.
The errand girls
store kohl in it.
Your chief
is from this flower country.

My lady's flowerlike eyes
became lovesick
waiting for his return.

17. The floating cranes

Thalaivi to thozhi:

The reed grows taller
than the shrub.
Its white flowers,
swaying in wind,
look like cranes
floating in the sky.

This is the country
of the chief who,
by going after new women,
makes my poor heart suffer!

18. Twin flowers

Thalaivi to the friends of thalaivan:

The reed sways
like sugarcane
in the company
of the dark-stemmed sedge.
He is from this farm country.

My eyes, like twin flowers,
began crying
when he left me
breaking his promise
never to leave me.

19. Like flowers dripping rainwater

Thalaivi to thozhi:

The white blooms
of the towering reed
nudge the buds
on the large mango tree
growing on the sand bank
whose blooms smell
like the body of a bride
after nuptials.

He hails from this country.
My eyes shed tears for him
like flowers dripping rainwater.

20. My loosened bangles

Thalaivi to thozhi:

The winged bug,
which has six tiny legs,
lays eggs on the lotus
with a hundred petals.
The tall, bamboo-like reed,
hollow inside,
swaying in the wind,
destroys them.

Thinking of the native
of this farm country
has loosened my bright bangles.

3. The crab

21. The moist eyes

Thozhi to thalaivi:

Mother, the thorny plant
close to the pond
grows thick and fast.
The spotted crab cuts
the stems of the water lily.

The chief of the cool lakes says
he'll give up his erring ways.
Yet why have your kohled eyes
become moist so?

22. His promise

Thalaivi to thozhi:

The spotted crab,
found in mud,
lives in its hole
below the roots
of the thorny plant.

The native of this land
married me,
praising my virtues
and promising never to leave me.

What happened to his promise?

23. A hostile god

Thalaivi to thozhi:

Mother, here women
   pluck flowers
or play with crabs
among thorny plants.

My lover, living in a town
   adorned with lakes,
   comforted me
and made love to me.
Now he has become
   a hostile god.

I don't know why.

24. Cruel country

Thozhi to thalaivi:

Mother, here the crab kills
   its mother at its birth,
and the crocodile eats
   its baby after its birth.

He is from this country.
If not, why should he jilt
the gold-bangled women
whom he has enjoyed?

25. The loosening jewels

Thozhi to thalaivi:

Mother, the purslane,
bearing lush green fruit,
is fed by rain
and the crab snaps
its red stems.

He hails from this farm country.
Enamoured of his chest,
the jewels of many women loosen.

26. The change

Thozhi to thalaivi:

Mother, leaving its mate
in the beautiful field
where *karandai* grows,
the crab cuts *vallai*'s soft stem.

He neither knows our suffering
nor that of others.
How did he change like this?

27. Woebegone

Thozhi to thalaivi:

The crab cuts
the ripe sheaf
of the strong paddy
from the fertile field
and carries it to its cool hole.

Thinking of the native
of this country,
why have you become
so woebegone
that your bright bangles
have loosened?

28. The malignant goddess

Thozhi to foster mother:

If the malignant goddess
residing in the drinking pond
is what caused
the sickness in her,
then why do
her bright bangles slip
and soft shoulders sag
thinking of the native

in whose cool mud
the crab leaves tracks?

29. The crabs are busy

Thozhi to foster mother
advising marriage to the chieftain
to relatives opposing it:

Mother, when it
begins to pour,
the farmers rush to their fields
where the crabs are busy
cutting the pale seedlings.

Though my lady
has tightly hugged the chief,
the freckles
on her mound still remain.
I don't know why it is so.

30. My lady's beauty

Thozhi to foster mother:

Mother, the crab
has long eyes
that look
like the buds of neem.
Close to its cool hole,
the paddy drops its flowers.

Why does my lady's
great beauty wane
for the chief of this land?

4. To the thozhi

The thalaivi speaks to her thozhi in the first six and the mistress speaks to *her* thozhi in the next four.

31. Is he not bound by it?

Greetings, my friend.
Close to the banks of the river
where crooked *marutam* grows,
my chief vowed,
witnessed by all our friends
bathing there,
to be true to me.

Is he not bound by it?

32. Wax on fire

Greetings, my friend.
For the chieftain visiting my home
for one day,
the women around him
would claim to have suffered,
like wax on fire,
for seven days.

33. The clamour

They say
that the chief is bathing
with many women
in the large waterfront
where the tall *marutam* grows
with each woman clamouring
to hug his chest
covered in cool garlands.

34. My faithless lover

Friend, live long.

Like the colour of the pollen
of the hollow-stemmed lily
blooming in our pond

my eyes have become lovesick
for the sake
of my estranged lover.

35. Love can be cruel

Friend, live long.
Once my dusky beauty
was brighter
than the stem of the lily
with its fibres peeled.

Now lovesickness
has eaten into it.

36. No chance

Greetings, my friend.
If my lover
were to forget me,
and my kohled eyes,
shapely like a fish,
were to be free
from lovesickness,

perhaps I too would succeed
in forgetting him.

37. Will he be true?

Mistress to her friend:

Greetings, my friend.
The chieftain of marutam
has rejoined his wife
promising never
to leave her.

Skilled in making
the women who love him cry,
will he be true to his vows?

38. He's ignorant

Mistress to her friend:

Friend, live long.
The chief is ignorant
of those who trust his word.
My body has stolen
the beauty of the tender mango leaf
and bright bangles
adorn my forearm.

Still, he left me crying.

39. He'll return

Mistress to her friend:

Greetings, my friend!
The chieftain of marutam
pressed my provocative breasts
to his own chest
when he made love to me.

My soft arms grow thinner
and though he has left me,
he is not really gone from me.

40. The honey trap

Mistress to her friend:

Friend, live long.
The bangles in my forearms glitter.
And my eyes glisten with tears.
Those who say
that he has abandoned me
to live always with his wives
in their hometown
do not know
the native of this land

where the lily blooms
nudged by the catfish
and holds fast the bees
come to taste its honey.

5. The wife's quarrels

41. Cruel like the crocodile

Thalaivi to friends of thalaivan
refusing entry:

Loveless crocodiles
eat their own babies
in his flower-filled ponds.

No wonder
golden-coloured love patches
grow on the bodies of women
who believed in his words.

42. Is she mad?

Thalaivi to thalaivan:

Chief of the town
that brings in new wealth,
Your sweetheart,
who wears excellent jewellery,
has begun to avoid your chest
broad as the Cauvery
filled with fresh floods.

Is she drunk
with too much toddy?

43. A country measure

Thalaivi to thalaivan:

The hatchlings,
copper in colour,
mount on the tortoise
which looks like
a huge country measure
and go to sleep.

Chief of the prosperous town,
your bard is a greater liar
than you.
He makes too many promises.

44. The hatchlings' hope

Thozhi to thalaivan:

In the sweet waters
of the immense pool
the hatchlings live
in hopes of seeing
their mother tortoise.

So does your wife
think longingly of your chest.
Chief, knowing this
act accordingly.

45. What colour is lovesickness?

Thozhi to thalaivan:

Chief, in the cold season
the water is cool and muddy.
In summer,
it is clear like sapphire.
This river is a jewel
to your town.

But my eyes know nothing
besides lovesickness.

46. Go to her home

Thozhi to thalaivan:

Not only for you,
even to me it is sweet

if you remain
at the home of the mistress
with a beautiful forehead
doing all her biddings
without being told,
instead of making
your presence here.

47. Why lie?

Thalaivi to thalaivan:

The sharp-toothed bard's daughter
carries a broad, big pot
filled with catfish.
In exchange,
the housewife fills
it with pulses from
the paddy-harvested fields.

Townsman of this place,
my friends who wear
such fine jewellery know
that you lie
as much as your bard does.

48. The marks

Thalaivi to thalaivan
refusing entry:

The young daughter of the bard
who is skilled
in casting the nets,
brings a basket full of murrel
in exchange for which
the housewife pours
paddy reaped last year.

Don't come over
here my lord
with all the marks
of the other woman
on your body.

49. An adroit liar

Thalaivi to thalaivan:

The long-haired daughter
of the bard,
walking gracefully,
gets a basket full of paddy
for a few fish.

The bard is an adroit liar
and whose beauty
are you going to spoil next?

50. Be like *vanji*

Thozhi to thalaivan:

My mistress
who bears you in her heart
is sorrowful.
Her kith and kin and I too
are grief-stricken.

Chief of the region
where the *vanji* grows
to a great height,
kindly grant her refuge.

6. What the thozhi said

The thozhi speaks in all the poems.

51. The tamarind

The sharp-nailed water hen
longs for its blue-tinted cock
to cure its lovesickness.

Your broad chest,
which, like the tamarind,
made the mouth water,
is no more a cure
to her sickness.

52. Don't park there

Chief of marutam,
my lady's fingers,
already red,
are made redder
by handling
the red-coloured *vayalai*.

Her eyes,
crisscrossed by red lines,
red lips and youth
are ready to cry
at the thought
of your chariot
parked before
some other house.

53. The frightened lotus

Chief, breaking the banks
the first floods of the season
enter the field
frightening the lotus
into blooming.

The gods that reside
in the bathing place
did not bring
about her disease.
Only the false vows
you swore to her.

54. Whither goes your chariot?

In the good kingdom of Pandya
there are stout chariots
and even in summer
cool water flows.

Your wife,
once beautiful like Thenur,
has grown thinner
and her choice bangles slip
because you dally with women
wearing garlands of reed
whom I fear to cross.

55. The truth is out

Chief, your sugarcane machine
answers the elephants' trumpet.
Your bards receive
chariots as gifts.

You once loved my lady,
beautiful as Thenur,
and abandoned her.
The dullness of her brow
proclaimed her
condition to all.

56. Empty vows

Where the bright lights
turn night into day
as in Chola's Amoor!

Her bright forehead has dulled
because all your vows
have proven hollow.
What good will be the vow
that you make today?

57. Not so beautiful

My mistress is beautiful
like the fire
that rivals the rays of the sun
or the lily
that blooms in Thenur.

Is the woman
that you frequent
beautiful enough to distress
someone like my mistress?

58. Women trouble

Huge rice heaps
big as a mountain
are seen
in generous Viraan's Iruppai.

You who pretend
to be troubled by my friend
beautiful as Iruppai
will also wear
the same look
to your other women too.
May you live long.

59. A balm

Chief of marutam,
Live long. And listen.
In the days past
I was the balm
to cure your lovesickness.
Now when my lady is forlorn
I am sad
I can't offer her any relief.

60. Don't come like a thief

Chief of the fields,
the water cock calls
its squawking hen
to cure its lovesickness.

You come at a time
when her large mansion
is fast asleep.
Aren't you scared
of her father's spear?

7. What the thalaivi said

The thalaivi speaks to the thalaivan in all the ten poems:

61. The ripe fruits

You're fond of
marrying many women
beautiful like the town
of *Mathi's Kazhar*

where scarred mango trees
drop their ripe fruits
with a huge splash
into the vast ponds below.

62. The Festival of Indra

From the sparse shade
the peahen,
its head like a small bud,
sends mating calls to its cock.

On the Festival of Indra
you paraded
all the women of this town.
Not content,
in which other town
is your chariot parked now?

63. The smelly otter

Full of lakes
where the smelly otter
has ribbon fish
for breakfast!

Even if my beauty
is completely lost, my lord,
I shall never consent
to hug your chest
hugged by many women.

64. Eyewitness

Surrounded
by a whirligig of women
you bathed
with your favourite
in the fresh floods
of the river!
Not just one or two
saw this but many.

Don't hide it from me.

65. Not ready

Chief of the land
with great rivers
where the water lily growing
in sugarcane field
feeds honey bees!

Don't embrace
my body which has
given birth
to your son.
It will spoil your chest.

66. Who stopped you?

My lord, not out of anger
I am asking this.
Answer without lying.

When you started your chariot
to your prosperous home
thinking of your toddler son,
who was the woman
that stopped you?

67. Your jilted women

Your current fancy is an idiot.
I hear she compares
herself with me,
no way my equal,
and brags of her beauty.

She is unaware
that your jilted women,
numerous as the bees
feeding on a flower,
have their bright brows
covered in lovesickness.

68. Can a lily become a lotus?

Native of the place
where at maiden dawn
the round-stemmed lily
blooms like the lotus.

Won't the woman
that you consort
show some restraint
though I do?

69. A doll

I saw your girl, Chief,
in the public bathing place.
Her kohled eyes
were bleary with crying
because the clay doll
she had made
was swept away
by the flower-bearing flood.

70. A devil, now

Feeding on a variety of fish
in the common lake
the stork rests
on top of the marutam
close to the farms.

Chief of the place
rich in water and wealth,
the women you consort
are pure and perfumed.
I am like the devil to you now,
my beauty
slack after childbirth.

8. In the fresh floods

71. Tongues wag

Thalaivi to thalaivan:

Your darling wears
tinkling bangles
that startle the passerby
and walks seductively.

When you swam with her
in the fresh floods,
holding her tightly,
it set a number
of tongues wagging.
Neither the sunlight
nor the scandal
that followed can be hidden.

72. The fresh floods

Thalaivan to thozhi:

With only the petals and leaves
of the lily as her dress,
love patches
beautiful on her pudenda,
long hair swaying,
kohled eyes like the lily,
soft-natured,

she came to the fresh floods
to be my partner in lovemaking.

73. A dress of leaves

Thalaivan to thozhi:

Her brightly-coloured
dress of leaves sways.
Her spotless jewels gleam.
When she dives
into water
the smell of lily
oozing honey
is all over the bathing place.

74. A peacock descending

Thalaivan to thozhi:

With her bright gold ornaments
softly shining,
when she climbed
the *marutam*
close to the river
and dived,

her perfumed hair was like
the feathers of a peacock
gliding down the sky.

75. Accept it

Thozhi to thalaivan:

Chief, an ancient *marutam*
in full bloom
grows close
to the large bathing place
full of flowers.

Many saw you bathing
in its cool waters
with your sweetheart
and spread the gossip.

But you won't accept it.

76. What made her shine?

Thozhi to thalaivan:

Long hair looking like the reed,
beauty spots on her
like kino flowers,
a bright-bangled young woman
swam with you
in the cool waterfront.

Many say that later she shone
like a goddess
to heavenly women.

77. The talk of the town

The mistress to thalaivan:

Chief, live long.
Let me tell you one thing.
I wished to bathe with you
In the fresh floods
in such a way
that the water
was whipped into waves
and we became
the talk of the town.

Go with me and not to your home.

78. Hold my shoulders

The mistress to thalaivan:

Chief, apart from a spear
with a leaf-like edge
and swift horses,
Killi has an elephant force
that could knock down
enemy walls.

The fresh floods
breaking the dam
have such a force.
If you hold the float
as you would my shoulders,
I'll swim with you
in the fresh floods.

79. Whose daughter is she?

The mistress to thalaivan:

'Bathing in the fresh floods
for long,
your eyes have reddened,
whose daughter is she?'
Saying so,
you grabbed my hand.

Whoever's daughter she is,
you may not know.
And whose son are you
that grabbed my hand?

80. The red eye

Thalaivi to thalaivan:

I shall not be angry with you,
tell me without lying.
Chief of marutam,
you lent your shoulders
to some virtuous women
and bathed with them
for long in the fresh floods
of the muddy water.

So long, your eyes
have become very red.

9. Lovers' quarrels

81. I love you

The mistress to thalaivan:

The skilled drummers
sup on the remains
of the white-bellied tortoise
left by the stork.

Chief of bowers and lakes,
You said to me,
'I love you.'

Your wife will be very sorry.

82. Beware of your lady's anger

Thalaivi to Bard:

Your lady was enraged, Bard,

to know
that the honey-sucking bees
which sat on the flowers
on the chief's chest
also sat on the flowers
in my hair.

83. Leave me alone

Thalaivi to thalaivan:

To the woman that you married,
you've done precious little.
At least be so kind
to leave me by and by

so that the bright-bangled women
are also known
to be the wives of the chief
with cool waterfronts.

84. The common pond

Thozhi to thalaivan:

Like the cool fountain
in which many women bathe
in the month of *Thai*,
hair decorated
in five different styles,

your whoring chest
has become common to many.
Just on hearing it
she'll be unspeakably angry.
If she sees it,
tell me,
what will she be?

85. The wild hen

Thalaivi to thalaivan:

The grating voice
of the wild hen
calls all its kind
to the common ground
where their caterwauling
swells to a roar.

Chief of the region
that brings in new wealth,
You do such deeds
that only boys do.
Won't those that see it
laugh at you?

86. The nestlings

Mistress to thalaivan:

The call
of the soft-feathered nestlings
of the white-headed crane
sounds close
travelling across
a wide expanse of fields.

Chief, it is difficult
for you to grace my home.
Go home to your wife
and be united.

87. She hates all

Mistress to thalaivan:

Wearing the bowl-shaped
paganrai on their head,
the rich cowherds
use sugarcane as stick
to make mangoes drop.

Chief, your wife hates all.
Will she make an exception to me?

88. My sister

Mistress to her friends:

My sister says
I am keen to keep the chief
whose land has
flowered fountains
and honey-seeking bees
coming to me.
Pretending
that he is unwanted,
I intend to prove
my sister right.

89. Not good as a woman

Mistress to the bard:

Bard, live long.
Why is the chief
whose common ground
attracts the honey-seeking bees
generous to my sister?

Not that
she is good as a woman
but for her good traits.

90. The chief and the bees

Mistress to the friends of thalaivi:

Did the bees,
fond of sucking
honey from many flowers,
get this trait
from the chief?
Or is it otherwise?

Unaware of things being so,
his son's mother blames me.

10. The water buffalo

91. The ebony buffalo

Thozhi to thalaivan:

The ebony-skinned buffalo
has serrated horns.
Getting down into the pond
filled with flowers,
he destroys the lilies.

She's the daughter
of marutam's chief.
Her garland is made
of sugarcane flowers.

92. Give your consent

Thalaivan to thozhi (within
the hearing of thalaivi):

The black-horned buffalo,
its eyes red,
gives its udder secreting milk
to its beloved baby.

If I am certain of getting you,
bright-bangled maiden,
I'll come to the town myself
where your father lives.

93. Bees buzz on her flowers

Thozhi to foster mother:

Herds of buffaloes
have grazed the fresh
morodam and *ambal*.

So, swarms of bees,
keen to taste
the honey of flowers
from a number of pools
buzz on the flowers
worn on her head.

94. Lotus blooms in fields

Thalaivan to his co-travellers:

The long-horned buffaloes
look like the braves
of the town
while their cows
have the contented looks
of their wives.
They wallow
in shady ponds.

My wife, whose brow is bright
and beautiful,
is the daughter of the chief
in whose fields lotus blooms.

95. Even in daytime

Thalaivi to the messengers:

The black-horned buffalo,
breaking rope,
grazes the long-sheaved paddy
at dawn
in the town rimmed by water.

Even in daytime
my chief has made me suffer
pangs of a rare affliction.

96. The blue and white lily

The messengers among themselves:

In the water muddied
by the slow-walking buffalo
the blue and white lily
grow together.

The daughter of the chief
whose town is rimmed by fields
makes a sweet bed fellow
to her husband
whose town has common fields.

97. Cool like the lotus

Thalaivan to himself:

The black-legged calf
of the buffalo
gets a scare
on seeing its mother's horns

entwined with
the white *paganrai*.

She's the daughter
of the chief who has many ponds.
She's cool like the lotus
that blooms there
and smells so too.

98. The long-horned buffalo

Thozhi to thalaivan:

The long-horned
buffalo wallowing
in cool waters
looks like a stoutly-built boat.

Chief, have your
father and mother
taken you to task
as much as this
gold-bangled woman?

99. Cure for lovesickness

Thalaivan to himself:

The foraging buffaloes
crush the nests of the ants
built on the bitter gourd plant
leaning across the paddy field.

This soft-shouldered woman,
daughter of the chief
with land rich in flowers,
shall be the cure
for my lovesickness.

100. The bathing women

Thozhi to thalaivan:

The bathing women
in the pond
unhook their bright jewels
and hide them
in sand mounds.
Foraging buffaloes
dig them up
with their horns and hoofs.

She is the daughter of the chief
of such a rich place.
Her speech is sweeter
than the strings of the harp.

NOTES

I. Marutam
Orampokiar

1. The wish list

1. Scholars conjecture that Athan might refer to a Chera King of considerable repute praised by Kapilar and whose full name is Chelva Katunko Valiathan and Avini refers to the subsequent scion who came in the same dynasty after Athan.

    Obviously this poem refers to the lush landscape but mixing up the fragrance of the portia with the smelly fish may point to the chief's libertarian life style.

2. The thozhi certainly wishes well, but there is a hint of fear that the thalaivan's love for thalaivi is on the decline. The pale water lily is presumptuous enough to compare itself with the majestic blue lily in the same way thalaivan equates the noble thalaivi with women of lower order.
3. The thalaivan's marital life has dimmed in happiness because of his waywardness and the thozhi wants to renew it.
4. The warning is obvious. The thalaivan has become a plaything for the mistress.
5. The crocodile eating big fish in the same waters is suggestive of thalaivan's carnality and his chariot parked before the house of the mistress reinforces the idea.

6. The thalaivan is extending the *kalavu*, the secret love, without making moves for *varaivu* (wedding).
7. Besides denoting the riverine lands, *marutam* is also known as arjun tree or India's pride. Italics is used only when it refers to the tree and not to the landscape. Taking the lady to his house is a legitimization of the love, an event coming after the marriage.
8. The swaying branches of the mango offer uneasy shelter to the peacocks and the thalaivan's inability to keep promises threatens the relationship.
9. '*Alar*' or calumny is something the thalaivi wants to avoid by marrying without delay. The smugness of the stork may refer to the thalaivan's extension of the secret love.
10. The fragrance of the mango buds and the smell of the fish tell that corruption has set in.

2. The reed

11. The purslane creeper embracing the reed and the thalaivan's extramarital affairs which sadden the thalaivi have connections.
12. The reed, worthless, and the sugarcane, a valuable crop, appear the same. The thalaivan's choices likewise are indiscriminate, resulting in the thalaivi's sagging shoulders.
13. The reed blooming in the riverbank shows that women who are less worthy are aplenty. Their professional activities keep them awake in the night while the village sleeps.
14. The reed as well as the mango grows in marutam. Making the right choice becomes obligatory.
15. Selby makes the reed companions to the women bathing in the river. The thalaivan is on the prowl, disapproved by the community.
16. The hollow-stemmed reed is used by the servant maids, low on the totem pole.
17. The abundance of reeds whose flowers appear like flying cranes and the burgeoning number of mistresses shows the proliferation of the unworthy.

18&19&20. The mixing up of reed, on the one hand, and the sugarcane and the mango and the lotus on the other, a recurring image, shows thalaivan's want of values. His promiscuity makes her sad.

3. The crab

21-23, 25-27. The crab, with its pincer-like claws, is busy cutting the stems of the aquatic plants in the midst of which it lives. The chief, in spite of his promises, continues his dalliances, saddening the thalaivi. *Karandhai* is globe thistle and *vallai* is creeping bindweed.

24. The crab and the crocodile have cruelty built in them. The thalaivan has the same predatory appetites.

28. Popular belief has it that the gods residing in the drinking wells possessed the girls who went to draw water.

29. The thozhi makes it clear in no uncertain terms the love between the thalaivan and thalaivi, especially to relatives of the girl opposing it. This is known as '*aratodu nirral*,' the disclosure of love at the right moment.

30. The crab lives in the muddy holes of the paddy field and has its food delivered right at its doorstep. The fertility of these farms has made the thalaivan prosperous which in turn has made him fickle in his affections.

4. To the thozhi

31. The *marutam* is crooked in its growth. The thalaivan who pledges eternal love in its shade has no intention of keeping his words.

32. 'The wax on fire' has such strong sexual intensity to it as to need no comment. Thangappa's translation attributes the melting to thalaivi (62).

34. The colour of the pollen of the lily is golden yellow which is also emblematic of lovesickness.

36. The thalaivi points out the impossibility of forgetting the thalaivan.

37. The mistress's speech made within the hearing of the thozhi is both a provocation and a very subtle comment on thalaivan's character. Marutam can mean the tree as well as the landscape comprising of farms and fields.
38. The mistress is no common whore but one who had the same longing and devotion of the thalaivi. She is a lover-mistress or *kadar parathai.*
39. The intensity with which the thalaivan made love to her gives her this certainty.
40. The jumping catfish which makes the lotus bloom and the lotus that holds fast the bug that comes to taste its honey are powerful sexual metaphors.

5. The thalaivi's quarrels

42. The broad-chested handsome thalaivan would have been rejected by the mistress only out of spite or drunkenness. The Cauvery is an important river in South India and the principal river to Tamil Nadu.
43. The hatchlings, sleeping on the back of the mother tortoise, is an image of protection and safety, something that is missing in the thalaivan because of his fickleness. The country measure is made of dark metal used for quantifying grain.
44. The tortoise lays the eggs and leaves the hatchlings to their own devices. Their longing for the mother and thalaivi's sexual longing carry the same intensity.
45. The colour of the water in thalaivan's river keeps changing with the change of seasons. But the thalaivi is condemned to suffer from lovesickness all the time. The thozhi very often acts as the spokeswoman of the thalaivi to such an extent that any distinction between them is blurred.
46. The thozhi chides thalaivan in harsh terms literally telling him to remove himself from her presence. It goes to show the esteem in which the thozhi was held.
47. The pouring of pulses in a vessel which held fish is a kind of corruption symptomatic of the thalaivan's libertarianism.

48. The murrel is a fresh water fish known to be highly edible. This poem continues the motif of the previous one.
49. The bard, singer and poet, is also an emissary of the thalaivan who is out to make new sexual conquests.
50. The tall *vanji* (Indian butter tree) offers refuge to birds and a similar protectiveness is expected of the thalaivan especially towards those who love him.

6. What the thozhi said

51. The broad chest of the thalaivan once made the thalaivi excited. Because it has become a common ground for the mistresses to play on, it has lost its attraction. The tamarind that makes the mouth water is a sharp image. Critics also point out that the desire to eat the tangy tamarind occurs in the post-conception period.
52. The red *vayalai* (purslane creeper), red fingers and red lips have obvious sexual connotation and the thought of thalaivan's chariot parked before other houses hurts her. It is also indicative of the beginning of the menstrual cycle.
53. The lotus frightened into blooming by the rush of flood waters has a hint of violence. The thalaivan's insensitivity to her feelings shows a similar violence done to her.
54. Comparing the beauty of a woman to the beauty of a prosperous town is consistently done in *Ainkurunuru* and other akam texts. *Thenur* is reputed to be a famous town in Pandya Kingdom. Selby gets it wrong when she makes the women with whom the thalaivan consorts as objects of pity rather than fear. The other poems in this decad make it clear that the mistresses of the thalaivan are contemptible. The thozhi cannot bring about a rapprochement between the lovers as she is scared of them.
55. The turning of the sugarcane crushing machine is indicative of the town's prosperity which breeds vice. Though the thalaivi wants to hide her sorrow, the pallor of her body betrays it.
56. *Amoor* was in the Chola Kingdom.

57. 'My mistress is beautiful like fire' has an uncanny resemblance to the Shakespearean sonnet 130.
58. The reference to Viraan who ruled Iruppai might refer to the Virally Malai in Pudukottai district in Tamil Nadu.
59. The thozhi helped the thalaivan in the days of *kalavu* or secret love.
60. This water bird is known for its guttural voice.

7. What the thalaivi said

61. Kazhar is believed to be a town located on the banks of the Cauvery.
62. The Festival of Indra for a god notorious for his promiscuity, provided opportunities to the chieftain to arrange dance and songs to his subjects, no doubt creating a Bacchanalian ambience.
63. The smelly otter eating ribbon fish for breakfast points to the thalaivan's licentiousness.
64. Bathing with a woman that one loves was a custom known to be literally, 'fresh flood play' or *pudupunal adal.* Normally the thalaivan does it with the thalaivi but exceptions are there.
65. The thalaivan, sexually restrained during his wife's confinement, can bear no more but the thalaivi is solicitous for the beauty of his chest. There is also a belief that the milk of the lactating mother may prove deleterious to the thalaivan.
66. The thalaivan's return home to see his loving wife and son was impeded by a woman who diverted his chariot.
67. The thalaivi's contempt for the mistress as well as the thalaivan's multiple sexual partners is evident.
68. The lily blooms in the evenings and the lotus in the mornings. A change in the natural order is indicated. And in the order of importance the lotus is infinitely superior to the lily. And the analogy explains itself.
69. A scornful reference to the tender age of the girl implying she is inadequate to the needs of the thalaivan.

70. The reference is to the stork feasting from the fish-filled lake and the thalaivan's promiscuity. Still recovering from the pains of birth, the thalaivi notices the roving eye of the husband.

8. In fresh floods

72&73. Shows thalaivan's nostalgia and also his desire for truce.
74. A poem notable for its exquisite imagery. Shows the thalaivi in all her majesty, playfulness and adventurousness. The image of the diving peacock is evocative.
76. The beauty spots (golden discolouration of the skin), usually compared with the kino flower, were very much coveted by the ancient Tamils. A beauty spot on a woman's breast was supremely tantalizing to them.
77. The talk of the mistress sounds pretty contemporary twenty centuries later.
78. *Killi* is the surname of the Chola Kings as in Nalankilli and Nedunkilli though the one referred to here is not clear.
80. The thalaivi's reference to the lending of thalaivan's shoulders and the mistress urging the thalaivan to hold her shoulders (78) are cross-referential.

9. Lovers' quarrels

81. The farm folk, low in social ranks, have to eat the leftovers of the stork. The thalaivi will have to be content with the thalaivan after he has been enjoyed by the mistress.
82. The reference to 'the lady' of the bard is scornful. The 'honey-seeking bug' is a standard image of the philanderer.
84. The Tamil month *thai* (mid January) is a cool season when virgins bathe in the early morning and fast. The five different hair styles are: hair in a knot, hair curled, hair parted, hair plaited and hair gathered in a bun.

85. The reference is to the 'caterwauling' of the wild hens and the thalaivan who spends most of his time in the hen house.
86. The stillness of the vast fields. The call of the nestlings breaking this silence to reach the mother crane. The thalaivan too is troubled by reports of the first baby talk of his infant son. The imagistic accuracy is amazing.
87. The cowherds use the sweet sugarcane as stick to make mangoes drop. The wife, according to the mistress, will misinterpret even well-meaning persons. How will she think well of her?
88. The thalaivi's charge is that the mistress wants to keep the thalaivan to herself but she cannot bring about it. The mistress responds saying that she did not attempt it till then but would accomplish it soon.
89. The carping of the mistress continues. Apparently praising the virtues of the thalaivi, she denies her any feminine charm.
90. The blame cannot be squarely laid at the doorstep of the mistress for the waywardness of the thalaivan. His own lechery is also responsible.

10. The buffalo

91. The ebony-skinned buffalo destroying the water lilies and the thalaivan hungrily looking at the chieftain's daughter who wears 'sugarcane flowers' make the sexual intent clear.
92. The buffalo giving its udder to its calf is not necessarily a maternal image considering the thalaivan's assertion that he will ask her father for her hand if she consents.
93. The buffaloes destroying the *morodam*, a variety of acacia, and *ambal*, the white lily, and the consequent migration of the honeybees to the flowers worn on the thalaivi's hair makes the meaning clear.
94. The long-horned buffaloes and their contented cows wallowing in ponds are flagrantly Freudian. The lotus blooming in the 'field' shows that the land is rich in water.

95. The thalaivan who visited the house of the mistress in the night has started doing it even in daytime making the thalaivi sorrowful.

96. This poem gives a rare utterance to the friends of the thalaivan. The blue and white lily growing together shows the sexual union of the estranged couple.

97. The black buffalo, its horns draped in white *paganrai* (Indian jalap flower) is like the red wheel barrow and the white chickens by William Carlos Williams. Long before Ezra Pound advocated imagism, the Tamil poets who lived 2000 years before have got it down pat.

98. Another cool image. A partially submerged water buffalo is being compared with a 'stoutly built boat.'

99. The buffaloes crushing the creepers on the way to eating the paddy and the thalaivan's assertion that the thalaivi is the cure for his lovesickness are analogous.

100. The sand mounds, the bright jewels of the bathing women dug up by the horns and hoofs of the buffaloes are explicit enough. It also indicates the prosperity of the land.

PART II

NEIDAL AMMUVANAR

The scene shifts to the sea and the landscape close to the sea. Correspondingly, the flowers, birds, trees and occupations too change. The crooked *marutam* (arjun tree or India's pride) growing on the riverbank is replaced by the *gnazhal* or tiger claw tree. The lotus is replaced by the purple water lily; the peacock yields its place to the storks and cranes and light grey crows. The fresh floods of the river give place to the roar of the sea waves. From a community of farmers we move to a fishing community. What remains constant is the passion between man and woman.

Out of a total of one hundred twenty-seven poems composed by Ammuvanar, except for four, all others are on the tinai of neidal. He has contributed hundred poems to *Ainkurunuru*, ten to *Narrinai*, eleven to *Kuruntokai* and six to *Akananuru*. Giving dowry as a practice is mentioned by him in poem 147. He is also known to be an originator of "linked poetry" (*totarnilai*) as brought out by the ten poems on Thondi (171-180).

11. To the foster mother

In the following ten poems the thozhi speaks to the foster mother.

101. There he comes!

Mother, live long. Listen.
Severing the lush green *adumbu*
and trampling the *neidal*,
the chief's chariot
is racing to be a balm
for the lovesickness
in your daughter's
kohled, flowerlike eyes.

102. Relief

Mother, live long. Listen.
Like the cry of the birds
close to the vast blue sea
the bells of his chariot
are tinkling sweetly
relieving our suffering.

103. Her beauty

Mother, live long. Listen.
Mastwood
and tiger claw
bloom together
in the cool seafront.

The chief of this place
suits her well
and her great dusky beauty
is rather becoming to her.

104. The midnight visitor

Mother, live long. Listen.
When our village
was fast asleep,
with the beauty
of his body dimming,
the chief used to come
swift in his chariot.
His son is the heir to this place.

105. Pearls wink

Mother, live long. Listen.
Pearls thrown by the waves
of the roaring sea
wink on the white sand.

The chief came
to the cool waterfront
and her forehead
blushed redder than gold.

106. The web-footed swan

Mother, live long. Listen.
The web-footed swan
of his country mistakes
the conch of the cool sea
for its companion
and tries to make love to it.

The exquisite body
of my mistress
is glittering
more than the conch.

107. Sleepless nights

Mother, live long. Listen.
Lovesickness clouds
the bright brow
of my friend.
She's grown thinner
buffeted by restless thoughts.

I grow sad
when she can't sleep
on hearing the roar
of the cool sea waves.

108. He loved them once

Mother, live long. Listen.
If the chief of the cool sea
in whose backwaters
the thorny plant blooms
leaves my shoulders,
what does it matter
that he loved them once?

109. The good time

Mother, live long. Listen.
The *neidal* blooms
thick and dense
and hides the water
of the outlet.

When the chief of this land
left my arms
why do I remember
on a number of days
the time that
he had spent with me?

110. How will the god decide?

Mother, live long. Listen.
'The chief on whose shore
the mastwood breaks
into golden flowers is mine,'
I say.

But the town says
something to the contrary.
Will the god of fate decide it so?
Long live the god.

12. To the thozhi

The thalaivi speaks to her thozhi in all the ten poems.

111. Life in separation

Long live, friend. Listen.
Fishing in the backwaters
that rim the town,
the baited hook of the bard
nets the pregnant fish.

Without the friendship
of the chief
or the power of penance
in my previous birth,
how can I live in separation?

112. Out of modesty

Long live, friend. Listen.
The chief
in whose dark backwaters
grow lush green *serundhi* trees
will surely come
on his own.

I forget
his words to me
out of feminine modesty.

113. His woman

Long live, friend. Listen.
Yesterday the village called me
'the woman of the chief'
in whose country
tall waves smash
the white sand.

On hearing it
my mother asked me, 'Are you?'
Softly I replied, 'It's me!'

114. Shall we go to his country?

Long live, friend. Listen.
I cannot see him hereabouts.
Shall we go to his country
where the sea storks
resting on palm trees
cry unceasingly?

(What the lady said within
the earshot of the chief)

115. The playmate

Long live, friend. Listen.
The chief of the cool sea port
who once played with me
on the fine sand
is now hidden
close to my home
for my mother
has made it out of bounds.

116. The troublesome evening

Long live, friend. Listen.
When evening comes
the blue flower
in the dark blue backwater closes
making me cry
and the morning
that comes is like
its harbinger to me.

117. Forget or suffer

Long live, friend. Listen.
The mastwood flowers
dropping into water
make pretty patterns.

It is a fate cruel
to those who don't forget
the chief of the sapphire sea.

118. I relented

Long live, friend. Listen.
When I saw
the unjust man today
I wished to be angry with him
and deny him
entry to my home.

Later, rethinking,
and out of pity,
I relented.

119. No love

Long live, friend. Listen.
With his interest
in miscellaneous matters,
the chief of the soft land
close to sea
has not sensed
my distress.

Clearly, he has no love for me.

120. Beauty regained

Long live, friend. Listen.
The saltwater enlarges
the dark sandbanks.
When the chief of shores
came looking for me,
my arms, grown pitifully thin,
regained their beauty.

13. To the thalaivan

(The following ten songs can be taken as what the mistress said to the thalaivan suspected of having liaison with a nymphet. Or the thozhi mocking the thalaivan for consorting with a girl far below his age.)

121. The wet flower

Did I not see,
chief of shores,
your girlfriend who dived
into the crystal clear waves
with the thorny flowers
worn on her head
getting wet
and who stood
in the shallow saltwater.

122. The stork question

Did I not see,
chief of shores,
your girlfriend
questioning the stork
about the bright jewel
she had lost
close to the tall sand hill.

123. The dive

Did I not see,
chief of shores,
your girlfriend diving
into the cool big sea
to the clamour of her
bright-browed companions.

124. Angry with the sea

Did I not see,
chief of shores,
your girlfriend, angry with the sea
for washing away
her clay dolls,
throwing sand into the sea
to drain it off.

125. The cry baby

Did I not see,
chief of shores, your girlfriend
crying so much
that her kohled eyes
turned red
for the cool waves
had swept away
her sand figures.

126. The bees' mistake

Did I not see,
chief of shores, your girlfriend
taking a dip
into the huge waves
of the cool sea
to escape the bees mistaking
her eyes for flowers.

127. Still a girl

Did I not see,
chief of shores, your girlfriend,
a garland of leucas
on her youthful breasts,
leaving your bejewelled chest
without hugging.

128. Playing the mother

Did I not see,
chief of shores, your girlfriend
giving her milkless nipple
to a lifeless toy
made of reeds
and trying to feed it.

Poems 129 & 130 are missing from *Ainkurunuru*

14. To the bard

The thalaivi is the speaker in the following ten poems.

131. The calumny

It'd be good bard
to be the darling
of the chief of a town
bordered by *thillai* trees
had there not been
a resounding calumny
going against him.

132. The gossip

Long live bard.
You say the chief loves me.
But in this town
full of mastwood trees
breaking into buds
there is a lot of gossip about him.

133. I can't help it

Bard, what am I to do?
When the chief of shores
went away from me,
my bangled arms
lost their beauty
and became thinner.

134. My beauty returns

Look here bard.
When the chief's long chariot
drawn by galloping horses
came back, my beauty,
like the tender leaves
of the mango tree,
also returned.

135. No contest

I won't be troubled bard
to meet his woman
who has full,
bamboo-like shoulders,
a soft, broad mound,
and eyes that look
like the lily.

136. Liar

You're shameless, bard,
for speaking so well
of the chief of neidal
who makes
my bright bangles slip.

137. Peace no more

Let me ask you
one thing, bard.
Have the women
who loved your chief
who goes in a stout chariot,
ever regained their past beauty?

138. The bard's duty

You've failed
in your duty, bard.
You haven't given me back
the chief of neidal
speaking harsh
words of wisdom.

139. You hurt me

By abandoning me,
you hurt me, chief.
And your bard,
skilful liar that he is,
has made a lot more women
lose their charm.

140. Bangles slip

Look at me, bard.
I must speak to you
of your duty.
When the chief
of waterfronts left me,
the bangles on my forearm
slipped down.

15. The tiger claw

141. I'm lovesick

Thalaivi to thozhi:

The *gnazhal* and *serundhi* trees,
standing on sand dunes,
spread their perfume.
The cool waterfront splashes
on me the seaspray.

I've become lovesick.

142. Get some sleep

Thalaivi to thozhi:

The tiger claw branch,
bent with flowers,
is home to many birds.

Tonight I won't think
of the chief of shores.
Let my eyes
get some sleep.

143. Hated now?

Thozhi to thalaivan:

Her soft arms,
enfolding you
under the tiger claw tree
in which the birds
raised such a ruckus,
once gave a lot of pleasure.

Why are they hated now?

144. A single bird

Thalaivi to thozhi:

Dense flowers bloom
in the orchard
full of tiger claw trees.
A single bird rests
on its branch
growing close to the shore.

For the sake of this chief
my great beauty
shows signs of lovesickness.

145. The wave

Thozhi to herself(within
the hearing of thalaivi):

The tiny-leaved,
large-branched tiger claw
standing on the sand bank
is encircled by waves.

The lovesickness
of my dusky friend vanished
with the arrival
of the chief of shores.

146. Compelling beauty

Thalaivi to thozhi:

The tiger claw tree
that grows on the sandbank
began to show buds.
Now the buds have broken
into blossoms,
their fragrance wafting
all over the shore.

The chief of this land
no doubt finds
my dusky beauty compelling.

147. A country as dowry

Thozhi to thalaivi:

When women
make do
with the bright leaves
of the tiger claw
for want of its flowers
to make
dresses for themselves,
the chief of neidal
gave his country
as price for this bridal dress.

148. Feel free

Thozhi to thalaivi:

You can sweetly hug
the chief that you love

and on whose shores
the overgrown branch
of the tiger claw tree
spreads its
sweet fragrance.

149. Look after her

Thozhi to thalaivan:

Chief, neither hurt
nor leave my friend
whose beauty spots
on her youthful breasts
look like
the flowers of tiger claw.

150. His mind is elsewhere

Thalaivi to thozhi:

The huge branch
of the tiger claw tree,
bearing sweet-smelling flowers,
is drenched
by pounding waves.

Even on the rare occasion
the chief of this place
makes love,
he makes me suffer.

16. The white crane

151. I'll not open the door

Thalaivi to thozhi:

Walking elegantly
the stork went to console
the white crane
whose fledgling had died.
Touched by its legs,
the eye-like *neidal* opened
and the smell of honey
was in the wind.

I'll not open the door to the chief
because of a relenting heart.

152. He doesn't love me

Thalaivi to thozhi:

Walking elegantly
the stork that went to console
the white crane
whose fledgling had died
cries helplessly.

The incessant roar of the sea
sounds on the miraged shore
whose chief is, as you say,
just and loving—to the dame
they say he'll soon marry.

153. She has made up her mind

Thozhi to the messengers:

The elegant stork
that went to console
the grieving white crane
over the death of its fledgling
began to comb its feathers.
They all fell in a heap,
for anyone to keep,
blown by the wind,
close to a sand hill.

Will my friend
with long and pretty hair
love the chief of the port town?

154. They lie

Thalaivi to thozhi:

Walking elegantly
the stork went to console
the white crane
whose fledgling had died
and stayed there.

What good will it be
if I rejoin the chief
when the whole town,
supporting him, lies?

155. I gave him a baby

Thalaivi to thozhi:

The elegant stork
that went to console
the grieving crane
whose fledgling had died
scattered the *neidal*
overwhelmed by grief.

To the chief
who moves
with the course
of the water
I once bore a baby
made of reed.
(Replying to the friend who counseled
reunion because of her pregnancy)

156. She is not convinced

Thozhi to the messengers:

The elegant stork
that went to console
the grieving crane
over its fledgling's death
scattered its red feathers
all over the shore
touched by grief.

To me
the chief is a lover
but to my lady,
something else.

157. Without his father

Thalaivi to herself:

The elegant stork
that went to console
the grieving white crane
over the death of its fledgling
stayed there
from morning to sundown.

My son, out of love for me,
is coming alone
without his father
who is the chief
of this clear coastal town.

158. The mistress suffers

Thozhi to thalaivan (refusing entry):

The elegant stork
that went to console
the grieving white crane
over the death of its fledgling
roams with its mate
in the groves
of the vast beautiful shore.

Chief of the cool sea port,
I saw my friend,
who looks like
a tender mango leaf, suffering.
Attend to her.

159. Return her happiness

Thozhi to thalaivan:

The elegant stork
that went to console
the white crane grieving over
the death of its fledgling
stayed hungry.

Chief of the cool shores,
I'll not beg anything from you
but, before going,
return the femininity
you've stolen from her.

160. Make love to her

Thalaivi to thalaivan:

Walking elegantly
the stork went to console
the white crane over
the death of its fledgling
and came to be
gripped by grief.

Chief, your mistress
has become very lovesick.
Make more love
to her than before.

17. The light grey crow

161. I deserve it

Thalaivi to thozhi:

In the vast seashore,
the light grey crow
seeks shelter
in the dark branches
of the mastwood.

I suffer from pallor
and my brow is dulled
for loving with all my heart
the chief of this port town.

162. False words

Thalaivi to thozhi:

In the vast seashore,
the light grey crow
eats its choice of fish
in the deep pool of backwaters
and seeks shelter
in the sweet-smelling grove.

The words of the chief
of this waterfront
have turned out to be false.

163. My bangles loosen

Thalaivi to thozhi:

In the vast seashore,
the light grey crow
sleeps through
the roar of the pounding waves
and falling drops of water.

As soon as the chief
of this waterfront left me,
the bangles
on my beautiful forearm
began to slip.

164. Poor choice

Thalaivi to thozhi:

In the vast seashore
the light grey crow
likes to eat
the small loach
from the dark backwaters.

The chief of this cool shore
has made me sad
and laid himself
open to gossip.

165. Promises

Thalaivi to thozhi:

In the vast seashore
the light grey crow
gorges itself
on small fish
in dried up backwaters.

The words spoken
by the man of this port
took away
the beautiful bangles
on my forearm.

166. Don't trust him

Thozhi (within the hearing
of thalaivan):

In the vast seashore,
the light grey crow,
mistaking the striped white cowries
for fisherman's net,
gets a scare.

Trusting the words
of this chief of shores,
the eyes of my good-natured friend
lost their lustre.

167. Still a kinsman

Thalaivi to thozhi:

In the vast seashore,
the light grey crow
feeds on catfish
in the dark backwaters.

The chief of this waterfront
might have
denied himself to us
but an old kinsman
he is.

168. Break her fast

Thozhi to foster mother
disclosing her lady's love:

In the vast seashore
the light grey crow
lays its eggs
in the interior
of the abandoned boat.

If the chief
of this cool waterfront
is gracious enough
this bright-browed young woman
will break her fast
drinking milk.

169. From tree to tree

Thalaivi to thozhi:

In the vast seashore,
if the light grey crow
dislikes sheltering
in the bright-flowered branch
of the tiger claw,
it moves to the mastwood
whose buds are breaking
into blossom.

Even after knowing
the truth of the chief's heart
why does my eye droop
in lovesickness?

170. Is he good?

Thalaivi to thozhi:

In the vast seashore,
the light grey crow
scatters the *neidal*
blooming on the banks
of backwaters.

If the chief of this seaport
is good,
why does my kohled eye,
looking like
a many-petalled flower,
droop in lovesickness?

18. Thondi

171. She is like Thondi

Thalaivan to himself:

Mixing with the music
of sea,
in every street corner
there's the beat
of the two-sided drum
in the city of Thondi.

Her ample shoulders
and bright bangles
beg comparison with this city.
She's the one
who has stolen my heart.

172. Who stole my sleep?

Thalaivan to his friends:

Bees hum
close to the cool shore of Thondi.

Like the roaring waves
I am unaware of sleep
even in night
as the bright-bangled woman
has stolen my heart.

173. Suffer like cobra

Friend of thalaivan to himself:

Whoever looks
at this perfumed,
dark-haired maiden of Thondi
will suffer like the cobra
that had lost its precious stone.

He will not know
sleep even in night.

174. Agreed at last!

Thalaivan to himself:

Her jewels are finely crafted.
Red lines run through
her kohled eyes.
Beauty overflows
from every part of her body.
I was vexed
with not meeting her.

She has agreed
to meet me close to the pond
where gods reside
and which is beautiful
and perfumed
like the city of Thondi.

175. Bring your friend

Thalaivan to thalaivi:

If you show me
your gracious favour,
my love,
carrying many features
which make you
like the city of Thondi,

bring your friend
who has shoulders like bamboo
and a fine brow,
walking slowly. Long live.

176. What was my mistake?

Thalaivan to thozhi:

You're blessed with a body
that has the freshness of a new leaf
and a soft broad mound.
Your friend has the scent
of a cool fresh flower
blooming in Thondi.

This bright-bangled woman
has sapped my manhood
and stolen my sleep.
What was my mistake?

177. Guilty

Thozhi to thalaivan:

The sweeping waves
embrace the tall sand hills.

Whoever looks
at her shoulders like Thondi
with its sweet-smelling flowers
spreading their perfume
will tremble,
though he has made no mistakes.

178. I can't live

Thalaivan to thozhi:

The sceptred king
Kuttuvan's Thondi
has many excellent features
just as I have.

If they don't make her
accept my love,
can I live just by
praising her shoulder and hair?

179. She can't live

Thozhi to thalaivan:

My friend has a small brow
and is much like
the music of Thondi
where shrimps writhe
at the shore
when crabs launch
an attack on them.

Chief of the cool shores,
love her
for she can't live without you.

180. Her womanhood waits

Thozhi to thalaivan:

My lady's beauty
is the same
as that of the port town of Thondi
where an aged stork,
unable to fly,
waits for the fishermen
to unload the fat-filled fish.

Chief, marry her with little delay.

19. The water lily

181. End the gossip

Thalaivi to thozhi:

The girls have kohled eyes
that look like lilies.
Finely bangled,
they have ample shoulders.
By nature truthful,
they play innocent games
or stage folk dances
on the white sand.

If the chief of this town
rimmed by sea is gracious to me,
life will be sweeter
in this noisy town.

182. A mortal

Thozhi to mother:

The one who has taken
possession of her
is not a god
with rare gifts.
He is a young man
wearing a garland
composed of lily
and sedge.

183. You are too soon

Thalaivi to herself(addressing
the evening):

Evening that leaves
the lovers helpless,
when the native of the forest
with its clusters of waterfalls
and tiny hills
and excellent farmlands
and cool shores left me,
you arrived too soon at noon
as if appearing
at your customary time.

Even if you arrive
in the morning
when the blue lily droops,
who's there to stop you?

184. Vaster than the sea

Thalaivi to thalaivan's
messengers refusing entry:

A muster of storks
probing for fish
in the backwaters
pushing aside the blue lily
rests on trees
close to the shore.

My lover's town
is adorned by sea.
But vaster than the sea
is his love for me.

185. Who are you looking for?

Thalaivan to thozhi:

Her lips are like the trembling
    petals of the blue lily.
Her teeth have the brightness
of the pearls of *Korkai* port.
Her mouth is red like coral.
The conch, sawn in circles,
    gives her bangles.
Her words are sweet
as notes from the harp strings.

186. Beware of the chariot

Thozhi to thalaivan:

Like a siege of cranes women dry
    their wet hair combing it.

Chief of this port town,
I've heard my mother say,
    'I've seen a chariot
    coming too often
    splashing water
on the blooming lily'
    and warned us,
    'Don't go there.'

187. Take back your dress

Thozhi to thalaivan (Refusing
his offer of dress of leaves):

Others wouldn't pluck them.
Even the girls
who come to swim
with me in the sea
wouldn't use
these medley of leaves
for their sand figures.
A few flowers are good enough
for a garland
but the rest of this dress
is of no use.

188. Lovely like the lily

Thalaivan to himself:

The birds relieve their hunger
feeding on red shrimp
in the brackish waters.

Like the lily
that blooms
at dawn
in the vast waterfront
of Pandya's *Korkai*,
my sweetheart's eyes
are beautiful indeed.

189. The sparkle returned

Thozhi to thalaivi:

Pollen that drops
from mastwood
below which blue lily grows
looks like gold
embedded with sapphire.

Friend, with the arrival
of the chief of this soft land,
sparkle returned to my eye.

190. He made me cry

Thozhi to foster mother:

The labourer, leaving aside
the cool and fragrant lily,
harvests the paddy
in the land of neidal's chief

who alone made
your daughter's eyes,
which resemble the lily,
drip with tears.

20. The bangles

191. Who was the thief?

Thalaivan to friend:

Wearer of conch shell bangles
on her long wrists,
beautified with flowers
blooming in backwaters
on hair that grows
thick and black,
dressed in the leaves
of the tiger claw,
rare as a nymph
residing in the hills,
she was the one
that stole my brave heart.

192. The boatman

Thalaivi to thozhi:

Roaring waves
splash on shore
rolling the conches.
Close to the cool shore,
where water churns
with a thundering noise,
he steers his boat.

My bangles,
which loosened when he left,
became fitter with his return.

193. Right size?

Thozhi to thalaivan:

On the long seashore
ploughed by *valampuri* conches,
the bright light of pearls
wink in darkness.

Chief, are the bangles
you have brought
sawn out of conches
better than the ones
she wore before?

194. Beware of her mother.

Thozhi to thalaivan:

Chief of shores,
The conch of the sea
cut with sword
gives her bangles
and a few other armlets.

Look at her state now.
Her fine brow has lost its light
and her mother looks
at her askance.

195. My sleep is gone

Thalaivan to himself:

Fishermen sell pearls born
in oysters.

The lovely daughter
of the chief of this shore
has given me such suffering
that finds no relief.
The sweet sleep
I got on my bed
has been stolen by her.

196. Marry her at once

Thozhi to thalaivan:

Chief of cool seashores,
red shrimp gets caught
in your clear backwaters.

Her bright bangles
are sawn out of conch.
As for her hair,
it is dense and luxuriant.
She has the choicest of armlets.
If you love this
young woman so much,
marry her at once.

197. The language of the eyes

Thalaivan to himself:

Her bright bangles tinkle
scaring the crabs.
Being coy,
she buries her face
in her own hair
and looks at me
with concupiscent eyes.

With this lonesome evening gone,
she'll offer her sweet breasts to me.

198. Buds open their petals

Thozhi to thalaivi:

Young women with bangles
covering their forearm,
and smiles displaying white teeth
play in this seashore
where buds open their petals.

There I saw our chief,
broad-shouldered,
asking the way to our jetty.

199. Let's climb

Thozhi to thalaivi:

In the groves
close to the seashore
the roaring waves splash
and retreat.

Let's climb
the sky-high sand hill
and gaze at the country
of booming waves
whose chief made
your well-fitting bangles loose.

200. Laugh it away

Thozhi to thalaivi:

Friend wearing
clear, thick, and bright bangles,
to restore the customary beauty
of your forehead
the chief has come
in his golden chariot.
Open your long eyes
across which red lines run.

Let's together mock
the lovesickness
that steals away your beauty.

NOTES

II. Neidal
Ammuvanar

11. To the foster mother

101. '*Adumbu*' or hare leaf grows close to the shore. '*Neidal*' is the water lily.
105. The forehead blushing 'redder than gold' and the pearls winking on the sand catching the sunlight are rich images.
106. The swan mistaking the white conch for its mate and the thalaivi's body outshining the conch are implicit sexual imagery.
107. The roar of the cool waves must have a soothing effect but it keeps the girl awake as it reminds her of her lover.
108. The shoulders that could not keep the lover close to her have lost their charm. In keeping with her prickly mood, the plant that grows is the thorny plant.
110. The god of fate who brought about their union will not be the one that separates them. The girl's consolation comes from this thought.

12. To the thozhi

111. The bard, who is also an emissary of the chief, cleverly ensnares the girl for the chief.
112. The vehement words of passion that the chief used cannot be divulged as they touch the core of her femininity.

113. Already a rumour is gaining ground that the girl happens to be 'the woman of the chief.' The girl is secretly pleased about it but cannot admit to being so to her mother. So she replies *sotto voce*.

115. To declare the girl to be 'out of bounds' is literally a kind of house arrest which would make it impossible for the chief to see her.

116. The evening, the right time for the lovers, has become troublesome to the thalaivi.

118. 'Denying entry to home,' besides its Freudian undertones, points to the marital rights exercised by the wife.

120. The beauty of the girl returns or disappears depending on the thalaivan's presence or absence.

13. To the thalaivan

121. The young girl, with whom the thalaivan is in love, exhibits all the insouciance and innocence of the teenager. Diving into the crystal clear waves with flowers still worn on her head shows this attitude which the speaker makes fun of.

122. Questioning the stork over a lost jewel tells she is hardly out of her girlhood.

124&125. She is prone to the temper tantrums of the child as evident from her angry reaction to the sea washing away her images.

126. The bees mistaking the eyes of the girl for a flower is a frequent comparison in Sangam literature.

127. Wearing a garland of leucas shows want of discrimination and her refusal to hug the thalaivan's chest shows her sexual immaturity.

128. Breast-feeding the doll made of reeds may show her latent maternal instinct but it also shows the girl with traces of girlhood playfulness.

129&130. They are the missing poems of *Ainkurunuru*.

14. To the bard

131&132. The *thillai* trees (Indian blind tree) grow close to the coast. They are also known as mangrove tree. The reputation of the thalaivan has taken a beating because of his dalliances.

133&134. The beauty of the thalaivi that went away in poem 133 makes a comeback with the return of the thalaivan. The reappearance of the tender mango leaves with the change in season seamlessly merges with the return of the beauty of the thalaivi maintaining an organicity between the natural and the human world.

135. The *neidal* is the pale water lily growing in the backwaters. The thalaivi holds her own and refuses to be cowed down by the latest fancy of the thalaivan.

136. The bard, coming as an emissary of the thalaivan, praises him extravagantly to the thalaivi who knows only too well how he was fooling around.

137. The thalaivan is a regular Don Juan and the women who fell in love with him have to bear the agony of his parting.

138. These words of thalaivi, spoken half-jokingly to the bard, conceals the fact that the thalaivan has already made his peace and returned home.

140. One of the duties of the bard is to see that there is peace between the lovers. A rift between them shows the bard in poor light.

15. The tiger claw

141. A love-lorn maiden. The tiger claw and the sedge (*serundhi*) are in bloom. Evening. The splashing waves send drops of water flying. A colour photograph with a high resolution camera could not capture the mood better than these lines.

142. The branch of the tiger claw, laden with flowers, sags still more with the weight of the water birds. Thalaivi's heart weighs heavily with thoughts of her lover. Her resolution not to think of him that night may not fructify.

144. The single bird resting on a branch perhaps looking for its mate is the objective correlative of the thalaivi's emotions.

147. The chief's offer of a country as the price for the dress of leaves shows his great love for the thalaivi.

148. With all obstacles removed from her path, the thalaivi can freely make love to the chief.

149. Shows how solicitous the thozhi is. And her pointed reference to the beauty spots on thalaivi's breast, something that every woman desired, tells that the thalaivan is lucky to have her.

150. The sweet-smelling flowers drenched by the pounding waves is in marked contrast to the indifferent lover that the thalaivan has become.

16. The white crane

151. The stork which does not forget to walk elegantly even while going to commiserate with the crane makes one doubtful about its sincerity. The death of the fledgling is a reference to the purported death of the love between thalaivan and his mistress, the stork and the crane, respectively. Opening the door or shutting it (*vayil nertal, vayil marutal*) to thalaivan seems to be a privilege the thalaivi enjoyed.

152. Polygamy and bigamy had been practised and according to Arunachalam Pillai in *Chorpozhivugal*, it was the dwindling male population on account of frequent wars that made it necessary (119) but the pain felt by the thalaivi is self-evident.

153. The reference to the stork's feathers and the thalaivi's long and pretty hair is apt. the unanswered questions are: Is the stork's emotion genuinely felt? Is the love of the thalaivan real?

154. The thalaivan continues in his hedonistic ways and the thalaivi feels, perhaps with enough justification, that he enjoys the tacit support of the town. So she refuses his truce offer.

155. The thalaivan shifting his home with the shifting of the water course may mean he is sexually mobile. The thozhi counsels the thalaivi to reconcile with him given her pregnant state but the thalaivi says that she had already given him a doll baby made of reeds during their days of puppy love implying she has enough fortitude to bear the pregnancy alone.
156. The thozhi makes her friend's scepticism clear.
157. There are instances of the thalaivan returning in the company of his young son which may silence the thalaivi from making any protests about his sexual conduct. The thalaivi dreads such a return.
158. The thalaivan could make even the mistress despair over him. The thozhi's reference to his mistress as 'my friend' is ironic.
159. The thozhi demands one thing that the thalaivan is not in a position to return—her lady's original feminine charm.
160. The thalaivi rejects the overtures of the unrepentant thalaivan.

17. The light grey crow

161. The light grey crow, seen in the coastal towns, has a small white patch on its neck and it feeds mostly from the backwaters.
163. The crow prefers to eat the lowly loach from the backwaters in spite of the vast shore with its abundant marine life. This is a commentary on the thalaivan's sexual behaviour.
166. Fishermen tie cowries in the fringe of their nets which the crow fears.
167. Catfish is a poor choice of the menu given their sharp sting. 'An old kinsman' is a reference to his being a lover in earlier births too.
168. An imagistic beauty. The rotting carcass of a boat becomes a refuge for the crow to lay its eggs. The thalaivan, who has reduced the thalaivi to a skeletal state, may yet be the cause of her happiness if he chooses so.

18. Thondi

Identified as Alapuzha in Kerala, this coastal town seems to have been a busy sea port mentioned by the historians of the past. It had the richness of all the four regions that made the poets wonder how one should classify this town. Comparing a bright, prosperous town to a woman of exceptional beauty seems to be a settled literary tradition in the Sangam literature.

173. The friend of the thalaivan, rarely given a chance to speak, comments on the beauty of thalaivi which has kept his friend in a delirium of love. Popular belief holds that the cobra searched for its prey in the light of the precious stone which it brought out of its throat and losing it could prove fatal to it. Another interpretation is that the love-bitten young man would feel the same distress felt by someone bitten by a snake, as he is not supposed to sleep.
174. Thondi was famous for its aromatic spices.
175. Meeting the thalaivi in the company of her friend would make it more circumspect.
176. Such explicitness may appear odd today. But Sangam ethics did not consider such compliments like this as out of place.
177. The overpowering beauty of the thalaivi could produce such reactions.
178. The thalaivan compares himself and his many achievements to the town of Thondi.
179. A public scandal is better avoided.
180. The 'aged stork' may refer to the elderly contemplating marriage to the thalaivi, a kind of arranged or forced marriage known as 'notumalar varaivu.'

19. The water lily

181. Life in the noisy town given to slander may be miserable to the thalaivi who wants to put an end to it by marrying. *Kuravai* is the name of the folk dance which is played by women cast in the role of husband and wife.

182. The mother usually mistakes her daughter's condition to be an act of possession by a god.
183. Evenings could be cruel to the lonely lovers.
184. The sharp-beaked storks stabbing the water and coming out with a wriggling fish may connote the sex act.
185. Korkai was a sea port in Pandya Kingdom famed for its pearls.
187. The offer of dress of leaves is a token of love.
188. These admiring lines are spoken by the thalaivan on his wife's skilful management of the household.
189. The thalaivan leaves the thalaivi mostly for reasons of making wealth or war.
190. Same as in 182.

20. The bangles

191. May not be the right kind of description to give to the Bureau of Missing Persons but very poetic indeed.
192. Riding close to the coast, where the waves are churning, the thalaivan wins admiring glances from his beloved.
193. 'Valampuri' is a rare kind of conch whose whorls turn right ('valam').
196. The shrimp getting caught and the thalaivan's readiness to marry are contiguous images.
197. Conveys the taut mood of the lovers who wait in anticipation of the sex act.
198. The buds opening their petals and the arrival of thalaivan at the jetty are not coincidental.
199. A glimpse of the thalaivan's shore will offer some relief to her.
200. The thalaivan's return drives away the blues.

PART III

KURINJI KAPILAR

From the sea to the mountains. From fishing to hunting. From the roar of the sea to the resounding noise of the waterfalls. From the heroine who waits for the arrival of the night on the shore to the heroine guarding the millets. Among birds we have entire sections devoted to the peacock and the parrot. Among animals the monkey and the wild boar figure prominently. The most important practice described is the *'veriyattu'* or the dance of the diviner. There is change everywhere except in the love that lights up every human heart.

For the sheer quantity of poems attributed to Kapilar, numbering two hundred and thirty-five, he is matchless. The breakup is as follows: *Narrinai*—20, *Kuruntokai*—29, *Kalitokai*—29 *Ainkurunuru*—100, *Pathirrupathu*—10, *Akananuru*-16, *Purananuru*—30 and *Kurinjipattu*—1. One hundred and eighty-nine of these poems pertain to the kurinji tinai earning him the appellation "Kurinji Kapilar." Praised by fellow-poets as a "brahmin of unblemished senses" (*pulan azhukkatra anthanan*), he is also known as "Kapilan whose tongue knows no lies" (*poyya navin Kapilan*). The friendship between the generous Pari and Kapilar is also legendary. After the death of his friend in combat, Kapilar too gave up his life by fasting but not before he got two of the daughters of Pari married as part of the duties of a parent.

21. Mother, live long

201. The magic mountain

Thalaivi to thozhi (within
her foster mother's hearing):

Mother, live long. Listen.
The buds that looked
like precious stones
became golden
when they bloomed.
He wore them
and gave me a dress
woven out of it.

What is this tree
that grows on his mountainside?

202. The tufted horses

Thozhi to thalaivi:

Mother, live long. Listen.
The horses of the chief
of high mountains
have tufts
on their heads like
our town's brahmin boys.

203. His water is sweeter

Thalaivi to thozhi:

Mother, live long. Listen.
The muddy water of his country
at the bottom of a pond
lapped up by animals
and covered with dead leaves
is sweeter than the milk
laced with honey
from our own backyard.

204. She is good

Thalaivi to thozhi (within
the hearing of thalaivan):

Mother, live long. Listen.
Like nymphs
of the mountains
the women in the village
assemble and praise me,
again and again,
wherever I go,
'She is good.'

But to the man
from the mountains
I've become bad.
Why is it so?

205. Her bed

Thozhi to foster mother:

Mother, live long. Listen.
My friend is very shy.
Scared of you too.

She likes to sleep
on the broad chest of the chief
from whose towering mountains
the silver fall cascades down
with a resounding noise.

I feel sorry for her.

206. A portrait

Thozhi to thalaivi:

Mother, live long. Listen.
Look there.

He stands like the guard
of the tank bund
during rainy season.
His bright sword
hangs like a garland
wet with raindrops.
The huge anklet is covered in moss.
Cool dew keeps his
waistcloth wet.

207. Rain, rain, don't go away

Thozhi to thalaivi:

Mother, live long. Listen.
Will drought
affect your field of millet?

Look there.
His tall blue mountain
topped by rain clouds
looks like meat
covered with fat.

208. Keep them in view

Thozhi to foster mother:

Mother, live long. Listen.
The kino tree fills
with its golden flowers
the broad pits
dug by woodsmen
looking for tubers.

Whenever the chief's
tall blue mountains
are lost to her view
my friend's lily-like eyes
are filled with tear drops.

209. The mountain reminds

Thalaivi to thozhi:

Mother, live long. Listen.
Whenever I try to forget him,
as you plead,

my chief's sapphire mountain,
on whose white head
huge rain clouds
like wind-blown
bean flowers
always rest, appears.

210. A cure for her

Thozhi to foster mother:

Mother, live long. Listen.
If she goes to our garden
and climbs on the fat stone
smelling of slaughtered animals
and gazes
at his bead-blue mountains
densely covered in flowers,

her jewels stay in their places
and the disease
that she suffers from
also lessens.

22. Mother

211. Wear it.

Thozhi to thalaivi:

Like the flour of black gram
mixed in ghee
and pressed into fine thread
the purslane grows
on the mountain.
On its beautiful top the *asoka* tree,
contrarily leaved, towers.

A dress made of these leaves
withers soon.

212. No reason to refuse

Thozhi to foster mother:

In the midst
of sandalwood trees,
the smell of burning logs
of white cedar.

He hails from this hill country
with its mixture
of aromatic smells.
If he is also just,
why should we refuse him?

213. My physician

Thalaivi to thozhi:

Friend, the sweet-smelling
tender mangoes fall down,
their stems broken,
from the scarred mango tree
like falling hailstones
and tribes living in dry lands
string them up.

If the chief from the country
of tall cliffs comes
I may yet live.

214. Grief giver

Thozhi to thalaivi:

Friend, on the mountain slope
a sweet and ripe jackfruit
falls from a cluster
into a fissure in the rocks
shattering a huge honeycomb.

The chief of this mountain country
is going to his place
leaving your large cool eyes
filled with tears.

215. What cruelty!

Thalaivi to thozhi (within
the hearing of thalaivan):

The bead-blue dragonfly,
in colour like the touchstone,
hums a song
sweeter than the music
of drum and flute
played at
the narrow bathing place.

He who leaves me
in this evening
when the bush
is in full bloom
is fit for acts
crueller than this.

216. A plucked tender leaf

Thozhi to thalaivi (within
the hearing of thalaivan):

Friend, the tiger with short forelegs,
an expert killer,
waits in the thick shadows
of the jackfruit-laden tree
to kill the shaky-legged calf
of a young cow elephant.

Why do you look
so woebegone
like a plucked tender leaf,
thinking of the chief
of such country?

217. He's here

Thozhi to thalaivi:

Friend, herds of deer
feed on the golden flowers
of the kino tree
on top of the tall mountain.

The native of the hill country
is here.
Yet why does your body
show signs of lovesickness?

218. The signs

Thozhi to thalaivi:

Friend, my finely-browed
eye twitches.
My downy forearm swells
and fills the bangles.
The tiger, angrier that the elephant
has escaped it, roars
which sounds like thunder
from the dark clouds.

Are all these signs
that the chief of mountains
is about to return?

219. Just for a few days

Thozhi to thalaivi:

The dark-trunked kino tree
sheds its
big-petalled bright flowers
beautifying the large black rocks.

Why does your bright brow
lose its lustre
as soon as
the native of the hill country
left your side?

220. A day wasted

Thozhi to foster mother:

Mother, the moving clouds
bring heavy rains
which swell into wide waterfalls.
They tumble down the hills
where swaying bamboo grows.

On those days
she couldn't make love
to the chief
whose chest is broad as a mountain,
her cool eyes, like wet flowers,
keep on dripping tears.

23. Thozhi, live long

221. A topic of discussion

Thalaivi to thozhi (within
the hearing of thalaivan):

Friend, live long. Listen.
My amazing beauty,
a topic of discussion,
is like that of a superb doll.
It'll soon be lost.
My body has a dusky beauty
and it'll droop in lovesickness

because my lover says
he's leaving for his hill country.

222. He seldom comes

Thalaivi to thozhi (within
the hearing of thalaivan):

Friend, live long. Listen.
The chief who came to our town
wearing a garland of cool
and fragrant flowers
and lived with me quite often,
seldom comes.

My brow, adorned
by lovely, dense hair,
suffers from love's pallor.

223. He is merciful

Thozhi to thalaivi:

Friend, live long. Listen.
The waterfalls begin
to flow from our hills.
The *kantal* is seen
in full bloom.

And before the onset
of fog and chill wind
which render
a lover helpless,
my lover came.

224. Too difficult

Thalaivi to thozhi (within
the hearing of thalaivan):

Friend, live long. Listen.
Close to the huge,
sapphire mountain,
in the crystal-clear fall,
it was easy enough for him
to enjoy a bath with me.

I'm afraid
it may be too difficult
for him now.

225. You must look your best

Thozhi to thalaivi:

Friend, live long. Listen.
Like the scent in the cool lily
which grows tall
in the midst of green foliage,
your hair smells sweet.
Your nature is soft.

Won't your lover think
of your beautiful forehead
showing strains
of lovesickness?

226. The honeybee

Thozhi to thalaivi:

Friend, live long. Listen.
Clusters of sweet-smelling *kantal*
bloom on our mountain range
bearing honey
which the bees drink,
and drinking it,
shift their place.

Your indifferent lover,
after stealing your stunning
and winsome beauty,
has come back now.

227. Do you still believe?

Thozhi to thalaivi:

Friend, live long. Listen.
He told us, plausibly,
'I won't bear separation'
and then left us
to live apart.

Don't you remember
the vow that he made
as your brow grows
paler by the day
and your sweet-smelling
shoulder thinner?

228. Life threatening

Thozhi to thalaivi (her relations listening):

Friend, live long. Listen.
The bright falls,
never drying up,
come down
from the tall hills
of his country.

If he leaves our town
without his plea
being heard,
what will happen
to our sweet life?

229. Has he returned?

Thozhi to thalaivi:

Friend, live long. Listen.
Did that loveless man
who had been gone
for many days
making us cry
return last night?

Your forehead glitters
with the winsome beauty of gold.

230. Good news

Thozhi to thalaivi:

Friend, live long. Listen.
He guarded the millet
along with you.
He made your soft arms
softer still.
He covered your brow
with lovesickness.

Your kin have agreed
to your marrying this man
from the hills
who left you long enough
to make your great
and golden beauty wither.

24. To the thalaivan

231. Heartless

Thozhi to thalaivan:

Chief of the tall mountains,
your parting has made
my friend with dense hair
and well-crafted jewels
lose her freckled, dusky beauty
and become pale with lovesickness.

How were you able to do this?

232. Impaired

Thozhi to thalaivan:

The natural beauty of my friend,
who wears flowers on her hair,
became impaired
when you left her
as you would a stranger.

Her jewels, bright like fire,
were drenched
by raining teardrops.

233. Don't go back

Thozhi to thalaivan:

You won't return.

The cold wind is cruel.
Don't go back
to your high, difficult-to-climb
mountain country
from where resounding waterfalls
bring down precious stones.

234. Dreams are sweeter

Thozhi to thalaivan (pleading
for marriage):

Chief, her lightning-like
jewels loosen,
she is growing thinner,
her fine forehead
shows signs of lovesickness.

She pines that your broad chest
she hugs in her dreams
she does not see
when she wakes up.

235. Congenial to lovers

Thozhi to thalaivi:

The sky which poured
cats and dogs
is without a cloud.
A time congenial
to lovers like this
rarely comes.

Will you make love
to the chief
to the tinkling of the chosen jewels
and vow never to part?
Or shall we go
with him at once?

236. Let's go

Thozhi to thalaivan:

Chief, my mother knows it.
The whole town speaks of it.
In my large prosperous home
loneliness torments.
The cold wind adds to our woes.

Shall we make preparations
to go to your place?

237. Where can I find you?

Thozhi to thalaivan:

Chief, driven by love,
and tormented by mind,
if I were to see you
in such a season, tell me,
on which side
of the towering mountain
does your village lie?

238. The good ewe

Thozhi to thalaivan:

Even if the long-horned ram
goes after other ewes
ignoring its mate,
the thick-haired ewe
bears life
hoping for its return.

Chief of the mountain country
with its large waterfalls,
every time you visit,
her beauty makes a comeback.

239. Rock it!

Thozhi to thalaivan:

In the season of *musth*,
the fluid that drips
from the spotted forehead
of the bull elephant
is drunk by winged bugs.
Driven by lust,
it mistakes a boulder
for its cow
and makes love to it.

Chief of the hill country,
if you don't come in time
to the softening
of her bamboo-like shoulders,
we might very well die.

240. Familiar smell

Thozhi to thalaivan:

I am not ignorant of it.
I know.
The beetles that have spots and lines
cluster on
her sandalwood-smelling hair.
The selfsame smell
now comes from your chest.

25. The exorcism

241. Will it become known?

Thozhi to thalaivi (within
the hearing of foster mother):

My friend,
you have sparkling teeth.

On seeing our acute suffering,
if mother summons the priest
to find the cause of it,
will he make our love
for the chief of the hill country
known to all?

242. The lover and the lunatic

Thozhi to thalaivi:

Out of ignorance,
thinking it's possession,
mother has become
deeply grief-stricken.

It's cruel to hide from her
that your kohled eyes,
lovely like lotus,
have lost their lustre
thanks to the lover
from the tall mountains.

243. Poor mother

Thozhi to mother:

Mother! If asked why her cool eyes,
beautiful like fresh flowers,
have lost their lustre,
the priest would say,
praying to the god of mountains
where pepper grows,
'It's possession.'

You'll also think it's true.

244. Praise him

Thalaivi to thozhi (within
the hearing of the foster mother):

Long live, friend. Listen.
Unless the priest
who comes to exorcize
the madness
sings in praise
of the chief's tall mountains,
their multi-coloured flowers
and sweet-smelling orchards
what good
will be his exorcism?

245. He is the cause

Thozhi to herself (within
the hearing of thalaivan):

If the aged priest,
coming from
the tribe of soothsayers,
rolls the dice
and determines
that the god of mountains
wrought her disorder,
then the chief
who gave her this sickness
must also share
the same affliction.

246. A denizen of the hills

Thozhi to thalaivi(within
the hearing of thalaivan):

The lifelike tigress
with dark seeds for eye balls
scares away the pests.
The tiger, emerging out
of its stony cave
where the pepper vine grows,
makes love to it.

The priest has made
preparations to drive away
her madness
which after all came to her
from a denizen of the hills.

247. Is 'Murugu' your lover?

Thozhi to thalaivi (within
the hearing of relations):

I know what made your mother
call the priest.

If he stands
at your beautiful mansion
and lifts up the talisman
and pronounces 'Murugu'
will it turn out to be
the name of your lover
from the hill country?

248. Simplistic

Thozhi to foster mother:

The porch is filled with sand
and beautified.
The volatile priest,
carrying the spear
that the god of mountain
bore in battle,
rolls the dice
and predicts the cause of her change.

If only her state is explicable
through such simple acts!

249. Let him live long

Thozhi to thalaivi (within
the hearing of the mother):

On the flat, freshly filled sand
the priest rolls the dice
and tells your mother 'Murugu.'

Let the priest live long.
Luckily for us
he's unaware
of the man from the high hills
and resounding waterfalls.

250. Dice tell no lies

Thozhi to dice (within
the hearing of the foster mother):

O Dice, you don't know lying.
In the sapphire mountain
the peacock dances
and sweet potato blooms.

Embracing
her youthful breasts
which bore the weight
of her ornaments,
a native of this hill country
has made her lovesick.

The mighty god of spear
did not bring about her plight.

26. The hillman

251. She cries like a waterfall

Thozhi to thalaivan:

If a member of the hill tribe
lets out a roar,
the dark cloud showers
droplets of rain.

On seeing
the fast-flowing waterfall
from your tall mountains,
my friend starts crying.

252. The timing is right

Thozhi to thalaivi:

Friend, the small hut of the hillman
has its roof woven by reeds.
The floating cloud,
ahead of its season,
hides it from view.

He lives in such a high country.
He came before the season
of quick downpours,
dense fog and sharp cold winds.
May he live long.

253. Maternal displeasure

Thalaivi to thozhi:

The hillmen burn sandalwood
whose smoke mixes
with the smell of honey
in the mountains.

If the chief of this hill country
marries me,
will my mother
too approve of it?

254. To the hill country

Thozhi to thalaivi:

The hillman chops
the sandalwood log
and burns it
whose fragrant smoke
envelops the *kantal*.

Bright-browed young woman,
honeybees hum
wherever you go.
The chief has agreed
to take you
to his country
rimmed by hills.

255. My sweetheart

Thalaivan to his friend:

She is the young,
lovable daughter of the hill man.
In appearance,
she is pretty like a mountain fairy.
Her breasts are like flower buds.
Her lips are red.
On her chest,
there are beauty spots.

256. She makes me suffer

Thalaivan to thozhi:

She is the affectionate daughter
of the hillman.
Bees buzz
on the flowers in her hair.
Cool leaves make up her dress.
Bangled,
she has sprout-like teeth.

Though young,
she makes me suffer
the torment of love.

257. How can you?

Thozhi to thalaivan:

The hillman prayed,
begged his god
and got this bright-bangled daughter.

Leaving her big, beautiful,
red-lined eyes
stained with tears,
you want to go away
to a country faraway from here.

258. Her agony will grow

Thozhi to relations:

The affectionate daughter
of the hillman
has the swaying walk
of the beautiful peacock.

If the chief of the tall mountains
is keen on marrying her
it's good to agree to this.
Agony will cloud
her beautiful brow
if you decide against it.

259. The hillman's daughter

Thalaivan to himself:

This is the woman
whose beauty torments
me: She is the lovable daughter
of the hillman.
She makes an offering
of a few kino flowers
and a handful of honey
to her tribe's mountain god.
Her hand is wet and scented.
Her body smells like *kantal*.
And her eyes
are tear-stained for my sake.

260. Not so easy

Thozhi to thalaivan:

The affectionate daughter
of the hillman
has soft shoulders.
Meeting her will be difficult.

She'll no longer come here
to drive away the parrots
on the green sheaves
for the millet planted
in this ploughed soil
is ripe for harvest.

27. The wild boar

261. Scared, is he?

Thozhi to thalaivi (within
the hearing of thalaivan):

The stern-eyed wild boar
has its fill of soft millet
and sleeps in the shade
of the hard rocks.

Your lover is afraid
of your father.
Is that why
he hasn't come?

262. Will he have a cure?

Thalaivi to thozhi:

The stern-eyed wild boar
eats the small millet
and rests with its mate
amidst the huge rocks
of the mountain.

The native of this
bright hill country
made me suffer
love's agony.
Friend, will he
have a cure for it too?

263. My beauty returned

Thalaivi to thozhi:

The ready-to-reap sheaves
of the millet look like
unblemished gold.
The wild boar,
having the colour
of the touchstone,
gobbles it till its stomach fills.

With the return of the chief,
my beauty too returned.

264. Look at her

Thozhi to thalaivan:

The wild boar,
its curved tusks
like the crescent moon,
makes love to its mate
dark as Indian currant.

Dweller of a country
with bright waterfalls,
look at the lovesick eyes
of the woman you love.

265. The boar is better

Thalaivi to the messengers:

The wild boar,
which has curved white tusks,
brings up its striped brood
after a tiger mauled its mate.

The chief of this hill country
has abandoned me
and my son
who is as good as gold.

266. You ought to be ashamed

Thozhi to thalaivan:

The small-eyed wild boar
launches itself
with great anger
against the massive tiger
with short forelegs.

Chief, we are bashful
by nature.
Is that why
you made the woman you love cry?

267. Seduction

Thozhi to thalaivi (within
the hearing of thalaivan):

The angry, small-eyed wild boar
gives the slip to the archers
standing on a range of small rocks
and has its fill of millet.

Knowing how simple she is,
he swears false vows of love
to the hillman's daughter
on whose flowered hair
bees buzz.

268. What good will it do?

Thozhi to thalaivi (within
the hearing of thalaivan):

In the company
of the motherless piglets,
after having its fill of small millet
growing on the fertile mountains,
the wild boar goes
to the mountaintop
where the woodsmen dwell
and sleeps it off.

If the chief of the hill country
goes away
leaving me alone
what good will it do?

269. Unfit

Thozhi to thalaivi (within
the hearing of thalaivan):

The reed grows like paddy
because the wild boar
with its sharp tusks
has upturned the soil.

Your bangles are beautiful.
Your hair is dense, even.
If the chief makes you cry,
I'm unfit to be your friend
for I lack understanding.

270. Lonely mountain

Thozhi to thalaivi:

The wild boar upturns the soil
digging for roots.
The woodsmen harvest
the first millet
from this loosened soil.

This tall, bare, lonely mountain
will make you cry.
Knowing this,
your lover has returned.

28. The monkey

271. An old friend

Thozhi to foster mother:

The female monkey
stuffs itself
with mountain beans
and bulges
like a shopkeeper's bag.

The chief can get
many women
like cows
from good families.
But being a lover
from her past lives,
he offers his love
to your daughter alone.

272. Cover of darkness

Thalaivi to thozhi (within
the hearing of thalaivan):

The black-fingered monkey's baby
grips its mother
without any tutoring.
The sweet honey
on the mountaintop
tempts it
but the swarm of angry bees
sends it scurrying
to the dizzying heights
of a tree's branch.

The chief doesn't visit me
under cover of darkness.
But my mother says
again and again
that he does.

273. She will cry

Thozhi to thalaivan:

The tousle-headed monkey's
strong baby
likes to eat on the way
the coral-red leaves
of the *asoka*.

Native of this hill country,
if you leave,
she who lives
only to love you
will cry more than I do.

274. Sleep snatcher

Thalaivi to thozhi:

The flame-coloured tiger roars.
Frightened,
the male monkey
bounds up the mountaintop.

The chief of the mountains
went away leaving me alone.
While going,
he carried away
the beauty of my arms
and my sleep.

275. Return the favour

Thozhi to thalaivan:

The leader of the monkey,
having distinct hair,
takes a short stick
and beats
the rain-born bubbles
showing on the broad rock.

Chief of this country,
we do love you a lot
and if you return this favour,
will our admired beauty
suffer so much?

276. Make her your wife

Thozhi to thalaivan:

The lover of the female monkey
has a taste for tender leaves.
He thrashes the young rain cloud
on the broad rock
using the *naravam*.

Chief of this country,
even if you don't love her,
let her be known
as the wife of the mountain chief
on whose rock
the kino blooms.

277. Eyes lack lustre

Thozhi to thalaivan;

Against the fat rocks on the porch
of the hillman's home
animals rid themselves
of their body's itch.
A male and a female monkey
gambol on such a rock.

Chief of the hill country,
let me ask you something:
why do you
have to leave her
making her lily-like eyes
show signs of lovesickness?

278. He makes us suffer

Thalaivi to thozhi (within
the hearing of thalaivan):

The baby monkey
swings from pole to pole.
The slender bamboo
straightens up swiftly
like a fishing rod.

My lover
is from this hill country.
He gives suffering
to the one who loves him
and takes away
her great loveliness.

279. Rife with rumour

Thozhi to thalaivan:

Climbing the *itri* tree,
which grows among rocks,
the male monkey and its mate
feed on the tender leaves
of the jasmine
and frolic on the mountaintop.

And my village,
nestling among mountains,
is rife with rumour and slander.

280. Happy tidings

Thozhi to thalaivan:

When the black-fingered monkey's baby,
untutored,
climbs up the tall bamboo
and playfully shakes it,
it looks like he is thrashing
the gliding moon
with a small stick.

Chief, I broke to her mother
the news of your marriage
as soon as I heard it.

29. The parrot

281. Long live the parrot!

Thalaivan to himself:

May the parrot live
long after many eons.

But for this bird
the hill woman of the sturdy arms,
bright jewels
and dark dense hair
wouldn't have come
to guard the millet field.

282. Take care

Thozhi to thalaivan:

Close to the mountains
the long-sheaved,
small-grained millet grows.
Though the large, cool-eyed
hill girl chides them,
the parrots do not scare.

Chief of this country,
do not come in this dense night
when tuskers roam
the jungle path.

283. Web of lies

Thozhi to herself (after thalaivi
has granted entry to thalaivan):

The stern-eyed woodsman's
soft-spoken daughter
drives away the green parrots
swooping down
on the millet.

Chief of this hill country,
though strongly counselled,
many a woman allows herself
to be caught
in her husband's web of lies.

284. Poor parrots

Thozhi to parrots (within
the hearing of thalaivan):

Pitiable are the red-beaked
green parrots
which keep returning
to the vast fields
of empty stalks of millet
after the hillmen
have harvested
for their love knows
no parting.

285. Hardhearted

Thozhi to thalaivan:

The hillgirl has a fine forehead
and plaited black hair.
After a repast of millet flour,
she chides the parrots
eating her grain
banging her rattle.

After you left her,
her bangles have come loose.
How can you be so hard-hearted?

286. A guilty spy

Thalaivi to thozhi:

After the millet harvest,
the bare white stalks stand
on which mountain beans grow.
The parrots now come
for the beans.

The chief of these fertile fields
is like one out to harm me today
by stealing
my dusky beauty.

287. Be true

Thozhi to thalaivan:

The short-legged goats
living on tall mountains
frighten the parrots
feeding on millet.

Native of this hill country,
you're an adroit liar.
But weak
in doing good deeds.

288. Thank you, parrots

Thalaivan to himself:

My heart knows
that the help they have given
is good.
What can I do to thank them?

Would the pretty,
soft-natured hill girl
have come to guard the millet
if not for the parrots?

289. One of their kind

Thozhi to thalaivan:

The hillman's daughter
sent to guard the millet
has a sweet voice
which makes
the parrots mistake her
as one of their own kind.

On seeing this
her kinsmen may call her back
from the task of millet watch.
Chief, marry her at once.

290. Like king

Thozhi to thalaivan:

The parrots seem to be
better placed
than the just and sceptred king
because the hillgirl,
her hair scented with bright flowers,
admires them
and chides them as well.

30. The peacock

291. Between mountains

Thalaivan to himself:

My love's arms
are like the bamboo.
Her pudenda sways
within her dress of leaves.

Her pretty village nestles
between mountains
where the peacocks dance
with the owls
taking turns to sing.

292. The woman you've married

Thalaivi to thalaivan:

The peacocks dance.
The honeybees raise
a mighty hum.
Cool rain clouds hug
the huge mountaintop.

Chief, the woman you've married
at her fine home
has made my virtue
shine forth.
She means more to me now
than you do.

293. Who else has this right

Thalaivan to thalaivi:

You close my eyes
with fingers like the *kantal*
whose scent
is all over the mountain.

Who else has this right
except the one
who sits in my heart,
lies down in my bed
with arms soft as bamboo
and has the looks of a peacock?

294. A worthy father

Thozhi to thalaivan:

The peacock sitting on the kino tree
with its flame-coloured flowers
has the look
of this bejewelled young woman.

Her plaited black hair
has flowers given by you
on this wedding day.
For this good deed
may your father live long.

295. Come back, heart

Thalaivi to her heart:

The forest fire
that the hillmen stoke
sends the peacocks
flying to their nests.
Sparrows living
in dry stalks
float like balls swatted
by hill women.

My heart that went away
with the chief
is yet to return.
Will it return or not?

296. I shudder

Thozhi to thalaivan:

The peacock living
in the mountainside
likes to steal
the long-sheaved millet
guarded by
the hillman's daughter.

Chief of this hill country,
You come
to see her in midnight.
What if the forest animals attack?
I shudder to think.

297. A peacock on the kino tree

Thozhi to thalaivan:

A peacock sitting
on the kino tree
that has burst into bloom
looks like a girl
plucking flowers.

Chief, you may part
from her
but she can't stop
loving you.

298. I cannot forget

Thalaivan to thozhi:

The peacock dances sensing rain.

My love that lives
in the good town
close to the small mountains
walks with a sway.
She may not return
my love for her
but I cannot forget
to think of her.

299. Matchless

Thalaivan to himself:

In the country
of the mountain chief,
the open-mouthed water lily
growing in the green pond
cannot match
the cheerful look
of the chieftain's daughter
with her beautiful hair
and swaying gait.
Nor can the peacock
claim to have her beauty.

300. Become better-known

Thozhi to thalaivi:

Like the long hair
of the hill girl
the peacock's feathers unfold
in the chief's tall mountains.

He has asked for your hand
and your kinsmen
have given their consent.
My sweet and soft-spoken friend,
may your good traits
become better-known.

NOTES

III. Kurinji
Kapilar

21. Mother, live long

201. The thalaivi's eulogy of the thalaivan's flora not only reveals her botanical curiosity but also explains her fondness for him.
202. Everything about the thalaivan's landscape arouses her curiosity, from trees to horses.
203. A poem often commented upon for the sheer intensity of love conveyed.
204. Even to the nymph-like women of the hills she is 'good.' A compliment rarely given by one woman to another. But to the thalaivan she has become bad.
205. The thozhi reveals the love of her friend.
206. A seriocomic picture of the thalaivan as seen through the eyes of the thozhi.
207. The mountains reddened by the setting sun and topped by dark clouds are compared aptly to flesh covered in fat. There is no reason for the thalaivi to fear drought which will prevent her from going to the millet field and the thalaivan.
208. The flowers filling the pit and the thalaivi's eyes raining teardrops are analogous images. The thalaivi cannot bear, even for a short while, the clouds obstructing the view of her lover's hills.
209. Even if she wants to forget, the rearing mountains won't let her.

210. The thalaivi's gaze at the thalaivan's hills cures her lovesickness at least for a while.

22. Mother

211. A dress made of the asoka leaves (mast tree) is given by the thalaivan as a token of his love.
213. The hunters living in dry lands collect the falling mangoes and preserve it till the next season.
214. A poem quoted to point out the fertility of the mountainside.
215. It is unthinkable on the part of the lover to leave his beloved like this. He who does it is capable of acts of greater cruelty.
216. The mountain teemed with wildlife and the thalaivan decidedly risked his life when he ventured out to see his lady.
217. The thalaivi is not yet aware of her lover's return.
218. Citing these favourable signs the thozhi tries to console her friend.
219. The thalaivi is unable to bear even a brief separation.
220. A day without making love is a day wasted. The clouds bringing heavy rains which swell into waterfalls have inescapable meaning.

23. Live Long, Friend

223. *Kantal* or malabar glory lily is remarkable for the way it looks like the fingers of a lady. To leave the thalaivi alone during winter months is an act of cruelty.
226. The bees shifting flowers after tasting honey and the lover who has had his fill are connected images.
227. The thozhi feels that the thalaivan is unworthy of her friend's trust.
228. It is unimaginable on the part of the lady to marry anyone other than the lover her heart desired.

230. No news could be more gladdening to the thalaivi than getting the acceptance of her kin to marry the man she loved.

24. To the thalaivan

231&232. The cruelty with which the thozhi charges the thalaivan was not present in the initial days of courtship. She wonders where he learnt the art of making a woman suffer.

233. Leaving the thalaivi as the cold season begins in the mountains is a wanton act of cruelty.

234. The sweet dreams of the thalaivi are in marked contrast to the reality in which the thalaivan is missing.

235&236. The thalaivi has decided on *utanpokku* or elopement as the last resort to marry her lover. It should be noted that the stigma which later came to be attached with this act was not there during the Sangam Age.

237. The thozhi speaks on behalf of her lady. She is an equal, confidant, often her guide and quite frequently a go-between in the best possible sense of the word.

238. There is a constant drawing of lessons from the animal world. The faithful ewe and the 'long horned ram' precisely reflect the human condition.

239. The elephant metaphor sublimates the human sexuality transporting it from mere lust to literature.

25. The exorcism

Summoning the priest to ascertain the thalaivi's sudden deterioration—the pallor, the love patches, the refusal to eat leading to emaciation, the dullness of the eyes and brow—has been traditionally done. It went by the name of 'veriyattu' or the dance of the diviner during the course of which the priest announced the cause of this illness. Usually he held the god of the mountain, 'Murugu,' responsible for the girl's illness. Sometimes he rolled the dice or 'kazhangu' (the molucca beans) on a level sand surface and tried to determine the cause. The thalaivi and the thozhi, who knew that it was a man who was responsible for this condition, generally opposed it. In the end the thozhi discloses her friend's love directly or implicitly, a practice known as '*aratodu nirral*.'

244. Hearing the praise of the thalaivan's hill or seeing a glimpse of it went a long way to mitigate the lovesickness of the thalaivi.
245. The thalaivan must share the blame in equal measure.
246. The thalaivi caught in the throes of lovesickness and the lifeless tigress comment on each other.
247. The thozhi is at her joking best. She is also making a disclosure of her friend's love.
248. The ancient practice of '*veriyattu*' is given in graphic details. Also shows the thozhi's contempt for it.
249. 'Murugu,' which means beauty, is the acknowledged god of the mountains and also the favourite of the Tamils among the pantheon of gods.

26. The hillman

251. The thalaivi crying at the sight of the thalaivan's mountains and the dark clouds showering droplets of rain shows the plaiting of the human and the natural worlds.
253. She is apprehensive about getting her mother's approval for her marriage.
255&256. The thalaivan's description of thalaivi conveys the aesthetics of the feminine charm.
258. The thozhi performs her office, i.e. telling the existence of the love between her friend and the thalaivan.
260. The millet being ready for harvest is good news to the hillman, but to the thalaivan it is bad, because he would no longer get to meet his love who comes to drive away the parrots.

27. The wild boar

The wild boar, though uncouth in appearance, is much appreciated by the ancient Tamils for its brave heart. It is habitually angry, easily provoked and would attack even a tiger if necessary. It closely bonds with its mate and if the mate meets with a premature end as in a fight with a tiger, brings up the piglets with a rare devotion. On the land ploughed by its tusk (it is looking for tubers) the farmers cultivate the next cycle of crops.

262&264&265&266. In contrast to the contentment of the wild boar and its mate, the thalaivan has left the thalaivi to suffer love's agony. In affairs of the heart, the birds and animals seem to be better than their human counterparts.

267. The wild boar could also be very wily as seen in the way it gives the slip to the archers. The thalaivan's seduction of the hillman's daughter is similar to this.

28. The monkey

271. The fat female monkey bulging like a shopkeeper's bag and the thalaivan's prosperity are interconnected.

272. The baby monkey's temptation to taste the honey is foiled by the angry bees. The mother keeping a stern eye over her daughter prevents the lovers' union.

273. The male monkey drops its aggression and runs for cover on hearing the tiger's roar. The thalaivan's departure withers the beauty of thalaivi.

274&275&276. The wanton act of destruction on the part of the male monkey and the thalaivan's indifference denting thalaivi's beauty seem related. It appears, however, that rather than looking for a strict one-to-one correspondence between the animal and the human world, it would be better to see how the analogy sets up a commentary on what follows. *Naravam* is a vine growing on hills.

277&279. The happiness of the monkeys is conspicuously missing from the human world. *Itri* is the white fig.

278. A poem frequently commented on its picturesque imagery.
280. The thozhi is not being nosy. She just cannot withhold her happiness. The happiness is also reinforced by the playfulness of the monkey shaking the bamboo pole.

29. The parrot

The parrot, fond of millet, is beloved of the lovers. It makes it necessary for the thalaivi to go to the millet field where she bangs the drum or rattle to scare them away. It provides a rare opportunity for the thalaivan to meet her in privacy and continue the *kalavu* or stolen love.

282. In a landscape teeming with wildlife, the thalaivan took such risks to meet his lady that the thozhi cautions him not to be so reckless.
284. It is obvious that the thalaivi is not only talking about the disappointed parrots finding the field empty but also about the clueless thalaivan.
286. The fields are so fertile that after the harvest of one crop another grows.
289. The thozhi uses all arguments to bring about the union of the lovers.
290. The thalaivi's attitude to the thalaivan is composed of chiding alone.

30. The peacock

292. The only poem in *Ainkurunuru* in which the thalaivi not only admires her rival but is also keen to have her under the same roof. Critics speculate that the first wife is childless.
293. The thalaivan knows from all available evidence that only the thalaivi could close his eyes that way.
294. The thalaivan giving flowers to thalaivi on the wedding day has the significance of stamping her status as wife as

only married women were known to wear flowers. (*Tamil Concept of Love*)

299. No lover has described the beauty of his sweetheart with so much eloquence.

PART IV

PALAI ODALANDAYAR

The thalaivan must separate himself from the thalaivi for the sake of earning wealth and apart from war, this happens to be the single strongest reason for separation in Sangam literature. Whatever be the reason, it induces sorrow to the thalaivi who could not bear to be away from her husband even for a short while. So the thozhi tries all available arguments to dissuade the thalaivan from going and sometimes succeeds but very often extracts the promise from him that he would return before the onset of the monsoon season. It should also be noted that palai, meaning desert, is not to be found anywhere in Tamil Nadu. It is only the mountainside and forest during the peak of summer when they appear to be desert-like. In keeping with the tradition of marrying a particular region to a specific mood, palai is synonymous with separation which in turn is connected to the harshest of seasons, the summer.

Odalandayar has composed a total of one hundred and three poems and excepting one, all describe the palai tinai. Besides the hundred poems he has contributed to *Ainkurunuru*, three more belong to *Kuruntokai*: 12, 21 and 229. Among the memorable characters created by him, one must mention the thalaivi who refuses to acknowledge the arrival of monsoon because her lover has not arrived (*Kuruntokai*: 21) and the mother who accepts the elopement of her daughter as ethical (*Ainkurunuru*: 371). Decads thirty-nine and forty of *Ainkurunuru* are especially singled out for praise as exemplars of his art.

31. Oh, don't go

The thozhi speaks to the thalaivan in all the ten poems.

301. She'll grieve

Chief on whose hilltops
clouds crawl,
those who walk in the hot sun
drape their heads
with the immaculate flowers
of the silk cotton tree.

If you cross
that mountain over there,
her grief would've grown
to a huge extent.

302. Don't go

Chief of the coastal town,
your efforts to make
precious wealth can go awry.
Your big-shouldered sweetheart
can also stop you.

It'll be good
if you don't go
leaving her crying.

303. Take us with you

Young man,
the fruits of the banyan tree
are of the colour
of a new earthenware.
Birds living there
have no need
to go anywhere else.

The dry land ways,
difficult to traverse
because of summer heat,
will become cool and sweet
if you take us with you.

304. The dangers

The untutored cowherds
dig waterholes
with their staff
from which wild elephants steal.

If you go
in these stone-strewn paths,
this soft-natured woman
with hair like rain clouds,
will grieve.
Chief on a galloping horse,
don't go away from her.

305. Learn from the elephant

A bull elephant,
assailed by ravenous hunger,
still makes love to its mate
without seeking
other pastures.

You want to cross the barren hills
leaving this bright-bangled
slip of a girl grieving.
What use will be your travel?

306. Cries like a flute

Victorious chief,
if you cross the vast dry land,
my dark lady—her perfumed hair
and bejewelled mound
losing their charm—will cry a lot
sounding like a flute.

307. It comes from her sorrow

The bamboos rub
against one another
and burst into flames.
The sound of this explosion
sends the tiger
bounding out of forest.

In this hot summer,
across hills and arid lands,
you wish to travel
to make wealth.
Chief of the shores,
this is not proper,

because it comes
from the sorrow
of this sculpted woman
who will suffer
from your absence.

308. Go when Murugan goes

If you never leave
this woman
who has dark, dense hair
and a gentle disposition,
it's good.

If you still wish
to leave her,
do so when Lord Murugan
forsakes this mountain
strewn with clusters of
strong-stemmed,
crimson-coloured flowers
of the *erul* tree.

309. They love you a lot

Chief, in this summer,
in order to make wealth,
you wish to travel
through the wilderness.

Is the wealth
that you make sweeter
than the smile
of your first-conceived son
borne by a woman
who loves you so much?

310. Her beauty will be gone

Young man,
beaten gold in the shape
of round coins
are strung together
to adorn her pretty mound.

If you leave her
after knowing well
that separation
brings down the bright bangles
on her soft arms,
you may rarely see
the beauty of her brow again.

32. The journey

311. Road less travelled

Thalaivi to thozhi:

Even if the girls
plucking kino flowers
sing dry land songs,
it frightens the travellers
passing through the forest ways.

My lover has travelled
such a road.
My heart fears he may extend
his stay there.

312. This blessed hill

Thalaivi to thozhi:

May the virtue
of this blessed hill
keep its bright waterfalls
always flowing
even when all else run dry
for it hid
my steadfast lover
from pursuing foes.

313. Love has turned burden

Mother to foster mother:

Listen.

Agonizing thoughts
assail my poor heart.
I feel my life ebbing.
Leaving all civilization behind
the daughter whom we loved
went beyond forests.

Let your love for her
be destroyed!

314. He forsook my arms

Thalaivi to thozhi:

The bright-bangled ghoul,
borne by her slave, whirls for prey.
The dark-eyed raven
and carrion vultures
circle the sky
making hoarse cries.
Small-eyed elephants
are out to trample the traveller
in this long jungle path
chosen by my lover
who hated my arms.

315. At war with themselves

Thozhi to thalaivi:

Our large eyes,
looking like flowers
with dew drops,
went to sleep
when he was with us.
After he left
they are at war
with themselves
but he is too far from here
to hear it.

Traversing dense
bamboo groves
he's left us
to the loosening
of our jewellery.

316. Signs of lovesickness

Thozhi to herself:

The string with its gold coins
that runs round her waist
has loosened.
Her mound, which is like
the seat of a chariot,
shows signs of lovesickness.

Close to the hot mountains
bare *omai* trees grow
and tigers stalk.
My lover has gone up
this forest path.

317. Missing heart

Thalaivi to thozhi:

Having lost all its charm
and greenery
the hot forest is changed
into bare dry land.

My heart
which has traversed
this harsh route
to reach my chief
has not yet returned to me.
Friend, let's find out why.

318. Beauty impaired

Thalaivi to thozhi:

The forest fire,
burning noisily,
scorches the mountainside.
The sunlit tall cliffs glitter.

My lover's passage through them
must be arduous.
Lovesickness has impaired
my rare beauty.
Sorrow has weakened me.
My full, bamboo-like arms
have thinned making
the stone-inlaid jewels slip.
He has extinguished
all my desire.

319. Harsh land

Thalaivi to thozhi:

Blinding sun.
Harsh terrain.
And trees
that are mere stumps.

Did my lover pass through
this pitiless forest?
Did he forget me
who never forgets him?

320. Agony

Thalaivi to herself:

The silk cotton tree,
with a spiny trunk,
shoots up
clusters of white flowers
which inflame
in the raging forest fire
and fall down.

My lover has gone
through this path.
While going
he left this immitigable,
unbearable agony to me.

33. During the dry land walk

321. The scream of the eagle

Thalaivan to himself:

The summer heat dries up
the eagle's head.
Its mate, with beak sharp
as chisel, sits on top
of the wide-branched *omai* tree
and screams out its loneliness.

Across dried up forests
and countries speaking
different tongues
and over mountains
I have travelled.
The sweet traits
of this bright-bangled woman
follow me everywhere.

322. Climate change

Thalaivan to himself:

The tall bamboo
turned into cinder.
The summer appeared
longer than usual.
The harsh rays of the sun
pulverized mountains.

It became too hot
to travel in the past.

Now, when I walk
with thoughts
of my bright-browed
young love,
the same route is cool.

323. I'm followed

Thalaivan to himself:

The sharp-toothed wild dog,
hiding among cacti,
waits to ambush
the wild boar
to feed its pregnant mate.

O my heart,
the sweet traits
of the lady you love
have followed me
all the way across
this harsh dry land.

324. Tormenting images

Thalaivan to thozhi:

Summer brings forest fires
along the interminable jungle paths.

Even if I close my eyes
for a short while
I saw her dusky beauty
flaring with freckles
the size of a kino flower,
hair with flowers dripping honey,
my big mansion in the cool plot

and the hum of bees
as the night closed.

325. My woman's traits

Thalaivan to thozhi:

The hot winds
of the summer
create a susurrus
of the peepal leaves
which frightens
the birds
and sends them flying
to some other land.

The heat of the summer makes
crossing the dry land difficult.
But my woman's traits
stood me in good stead.

326. Sweet woman

Thalaivan to himself:

In the hot dry land,
there's not even a patch of shade.
The mate of the young deer
with a fawn in its wake
is parched in the heat.
The floods have narrowed
the dry land path
making movement difficult.

But sweet are the traits
of the woman
I have left behind.

327. Cool relief

Thalaivan to himself:

The freckled and grooved trunk
of the small-eyed elephant
doesn't touch the ground
lest searing heat burn it.
The groves are reduced to cinder.
The tall knuckly bamboos
poke into the sky.

It's a path difficult to travel.
Only the thoughts
of my love bring cool relief.

328. No relief

Thalaivan to other travellers:

Excessive drought
has withered the orchards.
I have passed through
jungle paths.
Drops of rain
bring cool relief
with flowers
blooming everywhere
but I continue to suffer
from summer's heat.

I left my young wife
all alone at home.

329. A rebellion

Thalaivan to other travellers:

My stout heart refuses
to accompany me.
It wants to go back
to my wife
I've left behind.
She must be thinner now,
the armlets she wears
slipping down.

My heart has started
a rebellion of sorts
unwilling to go with me
through this vast,
harsh, desolate land.

330. She cries her heart out

Thalaivan to himself:

I've travelled far crossing
hot, dusty dry lands
and I wish to travel no more.

My wife, who likes
wearing bright armlets,
must be thinking
of the harsh country
I'm passing through.
She'll be crying
her heart out.
I'll travel no more.

34. The thalaivi's laments

331. Gone beyond it

Friend, live long. Listen.
The thick-trunked
cadamba tree bears
clusters of fragrant flowers
which I wear.
It grows on the mountain path
which my lover took.

Men who smell its fragrance
return home.
I fear he has gone beyond it
risking his life.

332. Dumb animals

Friend, live long. Listen.
The animals
that live in our forests
with its towering hills
are hard-hearted.

If not, they would've told him,
'Sir, it's cruel
to leave your love like that.
Please don't go.'

333. Did they forget?

Friend, live long. Listen.
The flocks of birds
in the hill country
through which my lover went
should've asked him,

'Sir, even birds like us
cannot live apart
from our mates.
How can you?'

I'm surprised that they didn't.

334. Devoted heart

Friend, live long. Listen.
The tiny-leaved gooseberry
grows closely.
My poor, devoted heart
follows my lover through
the sun-burnt stones.
My kohled eyes,
like blue flowers,
keep crying.

My lover's heart
has turned to a stone.

335. Feeding time

Friend, live long. Listen.
My lover returns
long after the appointed season.

I've heard it said
that the path he has taken
is full of vultures
with blood-red ears.
They wait to feed
on the stinking carrion
of some animal,
perched on the boulders
of the big mountain.

336. Heartbreak love

Friend, live long. Listen.
He made love to me
as if he could not think
of leaving me.

Now, drawn by a desire
for fickle wealth,
he has crossed
the sweltering wasteland.

337. Wealth is sweeter

Friend, live long. Listen.
We held each other
very closely and made love.
But clearly my lover felt
that wealth was sweeter.

Or why should he go through
the mist-covered mountains?

338. Adroit

Friend, live long. Listen.
Close to the mountainside
leafless silk cotton blooms high
which, catching the sun,
looks like mountain fire.

This is a season of togetherness.
But our lover is adroit
at leaving me.

339. No bats there

Friend, live long. Listen.
The neem has small leaves
and short branches.
The bats which love
its sweet fruits
throng the tree
when evening comes.

Is there no such evening
in the country he is visiting?

340. Doesn't he think of me?

Friend, live long. Listen.
Doesn't my lover
think of me?
Or is it that I'm mistaken?

He has left me behind
and the rumours fly
thick and fast
like the bamboo bush fire.

35. The spring

The thalaivi speaks in all the following ten poems.

341. Cuckoo's call

He has not come yet
but the spring has come.

The cuckoo calls its mate
in its sweet voice
across the rippling fine black sand.

342. Sweet scent of mulberry

He has not come
but the spring has come.

The mulberry,
which has a dark trunk
and large branches,
is in full bloom.
The wind wafts its sweet scent
and the hum of bees fills the air.

343. The fat buds

He has not come
but the spring has come.

The dense ironwood's fat buds
have opened up
in full bloom.

344. Toy figures

He has not come

but the season for girls
to pluck the sweet bottle flowers
which look like toy figures
has come.

345. The jasmine

He is yet to come
but the desirable season has come.

Across the wave-drawn dark silt
the jasmine shoots its tendrils
and brings forth its buds
which look like flowers
worn on hair.

346. The trumpet-flower blooms!

He has not come
but the time has come

for the red-eyed cuckoo
to announce
to the whole world
that the beautiful branches
of the trumpet-flower tree
have begun to bloom.

347. The beech tree blooms

He has not come
but the season has come

for young women
to make a paste
of the rice-like flowers
of beech tree and spread it
on their youthful
and beautiful breasts
to make them better-looking.

348. The oak blooms

He has not come
but the season has come

for the oak tree
to bring forth
its right-petalled
sweet-smelling flower
in our cool groves.

349. Flame-like tender leaves

He has not come
but the season has come

for the scarred mango tree
to bring forth
flame-like tender leaves
burying the branches.

350. Time for sweet nothings

He has not come
but the season has come

for the neem tree
to shed its bright flowers
and for him to whisper
sweet nothings
to bring me around.

36. Return of the thalaivan

351. Rejoice!

Thozhi to thalaivi:

My friend, your kohled eyes
have the look
of a many-petalled flower.
The travellers who go through
this rugged terrain
will have to content themselves
with the dried-up jackfruit
of the wayside tree.

Putting all his ordeals behind
our lover has returned.
Let your pretty mound,
sad all these days,
rejoice at this.

352. Smart lover

Thozhi to thalaivi:

The wild tribe
who wander in the forest
are skilled in archery.
The forest has stone tablets
for many a slain soldier.
This tablet has an exterior
akin to the skin
of an angry pachyderm.

Our lover has wisely chosen
to return to us than risk a passage.
Rejoice.

353. Fiery necklace

Thozhi to thalaivi:

The forest fire
drapes the mountain
like a fiery necklace.

The jewel on your lover's broad chest
has such a glow.
Crossing the mountains
with their vast orchards,
he has come
for you to make love.

354. Mellow mood

Thozhi to thalaivi:

The wild dog,
having made love to its mate,
is in a mellow mood.
On seeing the hind
with a fawn in its wake
it stops from giving chase.

Wearer of choice jewels,
spurred by his thoughts
about you,
your lover has crossed
such a forest.

355. Adieu to wealth

Thalaivan to thalaivi:

Wearer of well-made jewels,
in order to enjoy
your feminine charm,
I said, 'Adieu!'
to my desire to make wealth
and without telling others,
crossed the forest
where the freckled
and small-eyed elephants
were running amok.

356. Stopped in my tracks

Thalaivan to thalaivi:

The forest fire glows
like the golden rope
that the rich use
to string their elephants together.

Your soft traits,
sweet to reflect,
stopped me in my tracks
and brought me back to you.

357. The appointed season

Thozhi to thalaivi:

Friend,
the cadamba and the bottle flower
begin to bloom making
the rugged forest colourful.
Thinking that the wealth
he has made
is sufficient enough,
your lover is coming home
to restore
your dusky beauty.

358. Flooding tears

Thozhi to thalaivi:

He crossed many mountains
with tall peaks.

Won't your copious
tears—the more you wipe them
the faster they flow
like floods—bring him
back to you?

359. Return is swift

Thalaivan to thalaivi:

Driven by a desire
to make wealth,
I left you.
The path through the mountains
was long and tedious.

When I returned
by the same path
spurred by your bejewelled beauty,
it was surprisingly short.

360. The horses helped

Thalaivan to thalaivi:

My hind-eyed love,
the heat of the summer
creates forest fires
through which these long
and tedious paths run.

Yet my return was swift
because my heart was drawn
by a desire for you.
And the chariot pulled
by the galloping horses helped too.

37. You

361. Excellence

Thalaivan to thalaivi:

The jungle river
flows through steep sand banks
and has a large sand spread.
You plucked the trumpet flowers
which bloom in spring
and strung them into garlands.

Soft woman,
your breasts excel
your eyes,
your broad, soft shoulders
contest your breasts.

362. Surprised

Thozhi to thalaivan:

Chief, sweet are the flowers
of your garland.
The love that you bear
for my lady alone
has brought you here.

Neither the dark night
nor the want of a resting place
on the stony way could stop you.
You also braved
the small-eyed elephant
out to trample all its foes.
You surprise me.

363. Possessed

Thalaivan to thalaivi:

Younger sister of men clad in red
and who are deadly
with their sirissa bows
\and sharp arrows,

you think that the freckle
on your breast
to be merely a beauty mark.
To me, who is possessed
of its beauty,
it is a tormenting god.

364. Be patient

Thozhi to thalaivan:

Youth with a winning spear,
she is the younger sister
of the wild tribe
who have porcupine for meat.

Be patient
till I tell this dusky young woman
of your love
and get her consent.

365. Penance

Thalaivan to himself:

She drives away the birds
that come to steal
the fat meat
of the pack of animals
hunted by her brothers.

O tender mango leaf,
what kind of penance
you have done
to have the same beauty
of the huntress I love!

366. Just a bunch of flowers

Thozhi to foster mother:

Mother, live long. Listen.
Angry at my friend's sickness
you ask, red-eyed,
the reason for it
in a frightening tone.

I don't know anything
other than
what caused her thinness
is nothing more
than a bunch of ironwood flowers.

367. Conjoined souls

Thozhi to foster mother:

Mother, his garland had flowers
from the scarred ironwood
and for contrast,
clusters of kino.

When summer brings forth
colourful flowers,
he came driving a chariot
along the banks of the jungle river.

Her soul is conjoined to his.

368. Can she wait?

Thozhi to thalaivan:

The fire-like flower of silk cotton
blooms and falls
and forms patterns
in the dappled shade
of the beech tree.

My lord, if your soft-haired sweetheart
can wait without dying
till you return
you can have
the pleasures of spring
with me too.

369. Loud rumours

Thalaivi to thalaivan:

Chief, lush flowers grow
in the fountain
where the bees
hum a tune.

Many say
that you bathed with a woman
whose smile revealed even teeth
like sprouts.
These rumours sound
louder than the cuckoo's call
from the bottle-flower tree
in spring.

370. Don't hide

Thalaivi to thalaivan:

The lush branches
of the ironwood bear
sweet-smelling flowers
on which black-winged
bees buzz.

You lovingly made
a garland of these flowers
for her and lived with her.
Who is she?

Don't hide it from me.

38. Mother's laments

371. Right step

Mother to herself:

Let the peacocks
dance to the beat
of the hillmen's drums
and the tall hills
receive good rains
making her path pleasant.

My youthful daughter,
with forehead
like the crescent moon,
went with her lover
convinced
that was the right thing to do.

372. A thought for me

Mother to herself:

When she left
with the sturdy youth
convinced by his promises
a slander arose
in this noisy old town.

Would my daughter
have also thought of me
as she crossed
the fertile hills?

373. I curse his mother

Mother to herself:

The seasoned stag,
escaping the tiger,
calls its mate
in its distinct male voice.

In such a hot forest path
the youth bearing the bamboo bow
led my daughter away.
May his mother
suffer so much
that thinking about it
makes her tear-stained.

374. Too short for a knot

Mother to herself:

Even if I think
many times on it
it brings no relief to me.
Like the very god of death
the strapping youth protects her
in the dark jungle
whose measure not even
the male monkey has.

My daughter's hair
is not long enough
to gather in a knot.

375. Has she really left me?

Foster mother to herself:

This doll was sweet and pretty
to my own doll.
This green parrot was a pet
of my sparkle-eyed,
bright-browed green parrot.
Tears stain my eyes
every time I look at them.

Has she really left me,
my daughter with eyes like flowers?

376. Shaken

Mother to herself:

My large mansion
raised on righteous deeds
was reduced to tears every day
when my young daughter,
whose kohled eyes
were like blue lilies, left us.

May the unjust Fate
that made me suffer
suffer even more
like someone
caught in the forest fire.

377. The reminders

Mother to herself:

The thirsty elephant
lifts up its trunk
and trumpets its distress
which sounds
like a bamboo pipe.

The path that my daughter took
was through lands like that.
She left me as reminders
the ball and the doll
and a pile of molucca beans.

378. Poor companion

Mother to herself:

In this solitary evening
when the wide-winged bat
flits about
in search of fruits dear to it,

my grief is not so much
for my daughter
as for her heartbroken,
pretty-eyed companion
who longs for her sweet chatter.

379. Why did she go?

Mother to herself:

Is going with her lover
wielding a bright
and winning spear
through the groves
in the cold mountains
where an elephant herd roams
sweeter than the wedded bliss
amidst her loving friends?

380. I got a name

Foster mother to the relations:

I got the name of a mother
to my daughter,
who, known for her pearly teeth
and pleasant smile,
went with a youth
in the long path.

But those who gave me that name
were her own circle of friends.

39. During elopement

381. Mahanril birds

The travellers who saw the lovers:

Making a meal
of the green gooseberries,
sitting under the sparse shade
of the red-trunked cadamba tree,
who is this pitiable pair?

They are like
the short-legged,
wide-winged *mahanril* birds
which never know separation.

382. Mothers are pained

The women of a village:

The call of the strange birds
frightened her.
The sturdy youth carried
a polished spear
and wore a well-made anklet.
Crossing the difficult terrain,
they entered a small town
to escape the heat of the noon.
They created a stir
among folks who lived there.

Housewives with bejewelled daughters
looked especially pained.

383. Flowers for the doll

The onlookers:

The honey-seeking bees protest
when the young man bends
the short branches
of the tall cadamba tree
for his pretty
and long-haired maiden.

He is pleased
to see her plucking the flowers
whose petals move to right
separately for her doll
and for herself.

384. More beautiful

Thalaivi to the brahmins
travelling in the opposite direction:

Brahmins, your swaying walk
shows the keenness
to cover
long distances.
I beg to make a plea to you.

When you go through my town,
tell my companions
with soft forearms,
'Your friend's reputed beauty,
brought up
by her mother's loving care,
has become still more bright
as she trod
the difficult forest.'

385. Unjust mother

Thalaivi to the passerby:

'Mounting the long chariot
of the stern-eyed, strapping youth,
leaving behind mountains
with its man-eating tigers,
she has gone through paths
difficult to traverse!'

O blessed passerby,
please tell this to my unjust mother
who admired my arms
but who has lost her daughter.

386. Troubled woman

The passerby to the mother:

You who live
in a good and long-walled mansion
but have the scared look
of a troubled woman,

your first-born daughter
went with her lover
in the formidable jungle path
where tigers stalk
and killer elephants roam.

387. Joy unbounded

The brahmins to mother:

'Brahmin priests,
your tongue that chants the Vedas
also tells the ethics of living.
I pray you.'
So saying, ignorant woman,
you ask us the whereabouts
of your bright-bangled daughter.

We did meet your daughter
in the jungle path.
And praised by her devoted lover
she jumped over rocks
and climbed tall peaks
with boundless joy.

388. Directions

Passerby to the foster mother:

If you rest
in the sparse shade
of the black-trunked *ya* tree
to escape the fire-spitting sun
and climb a few small hills,
you will see the path
the girl bright as gold took
led by the youth
carrying a winning spear.

389. Solicitous

Foster mother to passerby:

Sir, you say
that you saw a woman
pretty as a doll, bangled,
walking slowly,
led by a black-bearded youth
wearing a well-crafted anklet.

Did her anklet-clad feet
touch the ground?

390. We did see her

Passerby to foster mother:

Madam, you who rush
to good men with folded hands
and your agitation
plain to see
ask the whereabouts
of your daughter,

we did see her
with a strong-shouldered youth
bearing a bow
in the jungle path.

40. Return of the lovers

391. Unblemished crow

Mother to crow:

Little black crow
of perfect feathers,
I shall offer you
and your loving kith and kin
food full of fresh meat
covered in fat
in a vessel made of gold.

Please keep cawing
so that my pretty-haired daughter
returns with
the fierce youth
bearing a formidable spear.

392. Don't pity

Thalaivi to thozhi:

Dear friend, don't pity these arms
once beautiful as bamboo
or worry too much about
my brow darkened by the sun
because I went with my lover
from the hills.

If you do,
it'll cause no end of trouble.

393. Has he returned?

Neighbours to mother:

You've grown thinner
from the day she left you.
And started cursing the gods
with tear-stained eyes.

Has your dear daughter returned
as a balm to your suffering heart
following the strapping youth
wielding the bright spear?

394. She's here

Foster mother to neighbours:

The unjust god
who had given me such sorrow
has now become kind.
My daughter,
known for her pretty hair
and eyes that make the hind jealous
and who took
the hot jungle path
has now returned.

Let me show you
the young woman
whose forehead looks
like the crescent moon.

395. Safety

Thalaivan to thalaivi:

Born in dry bamboo,
carried by strong wind,
the forest fire burns
like a long creeper licking
the fissure in the rocks.
We have crossed
that dangerous terrain.

And reached our mountain country
of booming waterfalls
and sweet orchards.
Young woman,
you can walk slowly.

396. The toast of the town

Thalaivan to thalaivi:

Let's walk slowly enough
to relieve the tedium
of this jungle path
and for me to pick
these kino flowers—they have
spots like the tiger's skin—and pin it
on your hair.

We have reached
our hill country.
Before sundown,
we'll be the toast of the town.

397. A message to my friends

Thalaivi to fellow travellers:

My fellow travellers
who hurry before me,
tell this
to my sweet, smiling friends:

'The wild dog
which has a downy mane
leaves alone the sow
with its brood of piglets.
Your friend has crossed
this jungle path
and is closer to town.'

398. Happy journey

Thozhi to thalaivi:

Friend, every time
I thought of you,
I wished you to find
along the path you travelled
such fruits that not even
birds have known
and such clear fountains
that not even deer are aware of.

Every time
I thought of you I cried
but more than me
our townsfolk suffered
for your sake.

399. A wedding for my daughter

Mother to others:

'Even if you do the anklet removal,
let the wedding proper
be done at her home,'—what
if you had told this
to the mother
of the sturdy youth

who carries a winning spear,
wears an anklet
of unblemished quality
and who is clever
in the art of lying.

400. Women are like vines

Foster mother to mother:

The stout cadamba
are erect as soldiers.
The women are creepers
that grow around them.

In this generous summer
with its abundant offer
of delectable fruits,
news of the return
of your daughter
along with her daring lover
who wears an excellent anklet
and carries a winning spear
has reached us.

NOTES

IV. Palai
Odalandayar

31. Oh, don't go

301. The tree mentioned here is *vellotiram*, a variety of cotton, whose flowers the wayfarers used to cover their heads as protection from the heat.
302. The thozhi is pointing out the futility of wasting one's youth for making wealth. (*Ilamai* or *valamai?*)
304. Thirst was a serious problem for the long distance traveller of the past.
307. Hot summer brought forest fires as the timber on the hills was bone dry.
308. Lord Murugan is the god of the hills. Selby attributes the leaving not to Lord Murugan but to the mountain itself (126).
309. As if crying wife is not sufficient inducement to stay, the thozhi introduces the toddler son.
310. Youth is fleeting, seems to be the message.

32. The journey

311. The journey through the forest way was one long and arduous trekking.
312. The thalaivi's elopement took her to these hills which saved the life of her lover from her hotly chasing kinsmen or marauders.

313. A poem which expresses the anguish of the mother in the clearest terms.
314. A catalogue of horrors that greeted the traveller through the jungle path.
317. Her fond heart is with the thalaivan and will return to her only with his return.
318. The poem begins with the burning forest fire and ends with the extinction of her desire.
320. The cotton flowers burning and falling in the forest fire and the agony felt by her merge with each other.

33. During the dry land walk

321 & 322. The eagle screeching out its loneliness across a barren landscape is a telling image accurately reflecting the thalaivan's state. But thoughts of his ladylove bring relief to him wherever he goes. *Omai* is the toothbrush tree.
323. The wild dog, which hunted in packs, is a vicious predator of the forest frequently mentioned not only for its ferocity but, surprisingly, for its love.
324. Images of his home and lady haunt the thalaivan.
325. '*Bogil*' is the generic name given to all birds.
327. The land becomes so hot in summer that the elephant keeps its sensitive trunk from touching the ground.

34. The thalaivi's laments

331. The fragrance of the cadamba tree usually succeeds in bringing back the thalaivan back to his wife.
332 & 333. Even the animals and birds seem to be conspiring against the thalaivi by not counselling the thalaivan to return home. The extended metaphor of birds, animals and flowers is intended to be illuminants of the human situation becomes clear from this.
339. The twilight brings out the bats known as 'fruit-eating bats' which throng the neem tree. The thalaivi wonders if such

things are there in the country the thalaivan is visiting to remind him of home.

340. The long absence of the thalaivan gives room to village gossip.

35. The spring

For sheer lyricism and sadness of the parted lovers, these ten songs of *Ainkurunuru* are unexampled. Within three lines, out of which one is a refrain, the poet packs a dense image conveying the thalaivi's longing. The thalaivan has assured the thalaivi that he would return home with the arrival of the early summer or spring, a season congenial to lovers. This is the season when Nature is at its best, with every tree and creeper blooming, much to the pleasure of the birds like cuckoo which welcomes it with incessant cooing. The joy felt by the animals and plants is missing from the humans as seen from the lugubrious lines spoken by the thalaivi.

341 & 345. The receding river leaves behind black silt and the water etches lines on the sand which resemble writhing snakes.

344. The bottle flower seems to be anthropomorphic like the mandrake.

346. The cuckoo, a rather elusive bird, did not seem to have escaped the keen observation of the poet.

347. Like the modern girls' fascination with creams and cosmetics, the girls of the Sangam had an obsession with their appearance.

348. The tender mango leaves have a colour akin to the complexion of the young women, a comparison all too frequently made in Sangam Literature.

350. The girl is obviously fishing for compliments.

36. The return of thalaivan

A walk through the desert-like landscape could be a tough ordeal. Lack of water on the way, the war-like tribe that infested the forest, wild animals like the elephant, tiger and wild dog and of course the weight of memories of his suffering love made the passage challenging.

351. The jackfruit, one among the three fruits known as '*mukkani*' (the banana and the mango are the other two) grows almost everywhere.
352. The stone tablets that dotted the landscape told of the fallen soldiers.
353. Frequent forest fires made crossing the jungle dangerous.
354. The wild dog was a feared predator.
355. Elephants running amuck are mentioned in many other songs too.
356. The golden rope of the rich kings keeps the elephants strung together. The invisible bond of love brings the lovers together.
357. The flowers often worked as clocks or reminders to the thalaivan telling him of the arrival of the appointed season. *Kuravam* is the bottle flower and *naravam* is the cadamba oak.
359 & 360. The return journey seems shorter because of the anticipated union.

37. You

361. Every organ of thalaivi seems to be an instrument of torture to thalaivan.
362. The thozhi is all praise because the thalaivan braved so many hazards.
363. A beauty spot on the breast of a lady was a mark of beauty to the ancient Tamils.
365. She does not guard millets as in *Kurinji* but the flesh of the animals hunted by her brothers. A change of occupation.

366. The butter cup flowers were offered by the lover about whom the thozhi is silent.

367. A mere look—in a flash—is often enough to bring the lovers together. Zvelebil explains this *iyarakai punarchi* (spontaneous sexual attraction) as "a union of lovers whose seemingly accidental meeting had been preordained in earlier lives" (*Lit. Conventions*, 3)

368. Though quite hypothetical, this is the only poem in which the thozhi talks about sexual union with the thalaivan.

369 & 370. These poems voice the suspicion of the thalaivi quite like the poems in Marutam. *Kongam* is a gum producing tree.

38. Mother's laments

The *utanpokku* or elopement was an option the thalaivi exercised when all other options were denied to her. It did not carry the stigmata which later came to be associated with it. Though her mother was anguished by her daughter's elopement on account of her tender age, it would be noticed that she did not condemn this practice during any stage of her sorrow. In fact, she devoutly wished for the return of her daughter—along with her lover. And secondly no mention is made of any unequal economic or clan-wise distinctions as hurdles for the lovers' union making many scholars believe that the Sangam Age was truly secular.

371. The peacocks dance in expectation of rain. The mother does not question the 'ethics' of her daughter's decision.

372. 'Did my daughter spare a thought for me, her poor mother or was her mind fully occupied with thoughts of her lover?' seems to be the unspoken question.

373. The stag draws the tiger to itself allowing its mate to escape. The mother is careful not to curse the son-in-law with whose life her daughter's is implicated.

374. Though the foster mother consoles herself, her real emotion comes out in 'My daughter's hair / is not long enough / to gather in a knot?'

375. The question 'Has she really left me?' hits like hammer. The reality is yet to sink in.
376. When she runs out of people to curse, she curses Fate.
377. The ball and the doll tell that the thalaivi is of a tender age. In *Tamil Concept of Love*, Manickam speculates that the girl must have just crossed puberty, i.e. twelve years of age.
378. The thalaivi and the thozhi were inseparable.
379. The mother could not understand why her daughter took such an extreme step.
380. The foster mother regrets that her own daughter, who is the thozhi, did not disclose the elopement to her.

39. During elopement

381. The *mahanril* is a water bird supposed to be inseparable from its mate. Elopement, with its privations, tested the resolve of the lovers to the utmost.
382. 'Housewives with bejewelled daughters looked especially pained' because of the pity they feel for the girl and the likelihood of a similar event happening to them.
383. Picking flowers separately for her doll and for herself shows the girl is not yet out of her playful girlhood.
384. The daughter is telling her mother not to worry about her condition.
385. The mother was not probably happy with her daughter's choice of husband.
386. The daughter's nonchalance is contrasted with the mother's trepidation.
387. The brahmins assure the mother of her daughter's happiness.
388. The foster mother who goes after the daughter is given picturesque directions. *Ya* is a tree mostly seen in dry lands.
389. The foster mother is solicitous about the tender feet of the daughter not touching the hot ground.
390. The foster mother's anxiety is plain.

40. Return of the lovers

The joy of the mother and the foster mother is boundless when the fugitive lovers return home. There is no harangue about the past. Only love.

391. 'The young man with a formidable spear' is not only a Freudian image but also shows the readiness of the mother to reconcile. Even today there is a belief in Tamil homes that the incessant cawing of the crows signalled the arrival of guests.

392. Thalaivi has returned thinner and darker after the elopement but she pleads with her friend not to make an issue of it as it would pain all.

393. No doubt the ebullience of the mother raises such doubts from the neighbours.

394. This poem may be thought of as an answer to the earlier query.

395. Forest fires were a constant threat in summer. The thalaivan assures thalaivi to relax as they have passed out of the danger zone.

396. The village will think of the thalaivi as a trophy won by the thalaivan.

397. The wild dog, a fierce predator, does not hurt the sow with its brood of piglets. A sentiment markedly absent in the human world which banished the lovers.

399. The removal of the anklet marked the end of the girlhood and the beginning of womanhood. This was done before the wedding proper.

400. While offering the good news of the lovers' return, the foster mother also points out the dependency of the girl on her husband.

PART V

MULLAI PEYANAR

The forest and the adjoining landscape, with the sweet-smelling *mullai* (jasmine) as its emblematic flower, this *tinai* has the thalaivi patiently waiting for the return of thalaivan who is at the battlefront. The monsoon adds to the woes of the lovers.

Barring the one in *Kuruntokai*, the hundred and three poems of Peyanar have mullai as their tinai. The decad forty-one "The Report of the Foster Mother" is adjudged to be his best which celebrates domestic bliss and harmony. The thalaivan seeing a vision of his ladylove in the dry land walk and the peremptory words of the bard to the thalaivan for remaining unmoved at the plight of his beloved are among his unforgettable creations.

41. The foster mother's report

The foster mother tells the mother what she saw in the
daughter's house.

401. Such bliss

Like a fawn
that lies
between the stag and its mate,
their son sleeps between them.

Such bliss like this
is rarely found
on this earth
covered by the vast blue sky
or in the world above.

402. Sweeter than harp

The mother hugs
her baby son.
The father hugs
her from behind
with desire.

This is a scene sweet
as the music
of the bard's harp.
It shows their goodness too.

403. Father's love

On seeing
the gap-toothed smile
of his toddler son
who bears
his father's great name
driving a toy chariot,
the chief's love
for his beloved wife extended
to his son too.

404. The bond

Cool forests
with fragrant flowers
and small hills adorn his country.
The chief of this pastoral land
hugs his bright-browed
young wife from behind
as she gives her nipple
to her infant son.

405. Lamp of her household

The roaring rain
has brought forth
multi-coloured flowers
in the land of mullai's chief.

Like the bright red flame
of the *pandil* lamp
the mother of his son
has become
the light of her household.

406. Play time

Winged bees,
drawn by
honeyed flowers,
raise a loud buzz
in the land of mullai's chief.

His lovable, kohl-eyed son
plays close by
while the chief
is in dalliance
with his sweetheart.

407. Domestic pleasures

Making love
to the woman he loves,
enjoying it
as one enjoys
the music of the bard,
the chief of the pastoral
lay in the midst of marital bliss.

408. Contentment

Bards played
the music of mullai
and his bright-browed,
bejewelled wife
wore jasmine.
Sweet was the time
our tall chief spent
with his son
whose innocence dispelled
all ill-feelings.

409. Sweet scene

Father hugged his son
whose baby talk
was sweet.
The mother hugged them both.
Sweetly did they all sleep,
a scene worth the wide world.

410. A cherished moment

On a joyful evening
at his porch,
in the short-legged cot,
the chief lay
with his wife-turned-lover.
Tickled by his son
crawling on his chest,
he chuckled.

The soft melancholy
of the bard's harp
wasn't apt for a time like this.

42. The thalaivan returns before the monsoon

411. Begins with a bang

Thalaivan to thalaivi:

My long and black-haired beauty,
the thundering black clouds
have brought torrential rains
in our enchanting forest.
The season of monsoon
has begun with a bang.

Let's rejoice
in these fresh floods. Hurry up.

412. Let's play

Thalaivan to thalaivi:

My large-eyed love,
The ironwood, laburnum, water lily
and varieties of wild jasmine
are in full bloom.
The forest is awash
with flowers
of breath-taking beauty.

Come, make haste. Let's sport.

413. Just like you

Thalaivan to thalaivi:

My noble love,
your forehead smells
just like the cool jasmine
growing in the forest.
The peacocks dance
just as you do.
The monsoon has set
as we desired.

414. Bucolic

Thalaivan to thalaivi:

My gentle love,
birds and beasts
make love
to their mates and frolic.
On branches and creepers
flowers of many kinds abound.
See, how sweet the fertile forest smells!

415. Time, place, love

Thalaivan to thalaivi:

My darling,
this is the season we desired.
That, my love,
is the forest we desired.
Sweet it is
when you are with me.
And sweet will be youth
if lovers make love.

416. Lovers' spot

Thalaivan to himself (within
the hearing of thalaivi):

Winged bees,
covered in pollen,
look prettier than before.
Drunk with honey,
their collective hum
swells to a roar.
In such a lovers' spot,
the elephant made love
to its cow
and I to my youthful love.

417. She made love to me

Thalaivan to himself (within
the hearing of thalaivi):

The monsoon mated
with the forest.
The forest grew festive.
My lady's beauty returned
with my own homecoming.
The fresh flowers
worn on her hair
drew a swarm of bees to them
as she made love to me.

418. Are you astral?

Thalaivan to thalaivi:

The sky,
taking pity on the skylark
starved of food,
rains without break
in the pastoral land.

You who made love
with your superb breasts
bearing down on me,
are you an astral being?

419. Animal love

Thalaivan to thalaivi:

These animals of the forest,
which know no separation,
mingle their souls and form
blameless friendships.
Look, my darling,
their lovemaking
is always intense
just as ours is in this forest!

420. I'll be back

Thalaivan addressing the forest:

The laburnum blooms
like bright gold.
The ironwood looks
like precious stone.
The malabar lily makes
the landscape prettier.

Forest, I've come to see you
with my bright-browed love
to reclaim her past beauty.

43. The miscellany

421. Persuasive

The neighbours:

The guards fling their silvery sticks
in evenings
and rabbits,
hidden behind
the sweet jasmine bushes, scamper.

The youthful daughter
of the forest chief
has pretty and persuasive arms
whose charm stopped him
from going on his travels.

422. Won't grieve longer

Thalaivan to charioteer:

My long chariot
is made of stout wood.
The horses that draw it
have sturdy legs.

If we ride fast enough
scattering
the white and red jasmine,
my love,
wearing armful of bangles,
won't grieve.

423. Can't bear separation

Thozhi to thalaivan:

The monsoon has brought
huge rains and thunder.

You have chosen to travel now,
making her bright brow
sick with pallor.
We have no strength
to bear this separation.
Her kohled eyes
looking like flowers
are brimming with tears.

424. Sadness all around

Thozhi to thalaivan:

Chief, if you go,
the adorable daughter
of mullai's chief
will have her
bright brow covered in
the pallor of lovesickness.
Your endearing son,
who looks like a lotus
in full bloom
in a clear pool,
will cry
for his mother's breast.

425. It'll be easy for me

Thalaivan to charioteer:

The peahen of the pastoral,
to the pleasure
of its cock,
makes a noise that resembles
the sweet music
of the king's singers.

If you drive my long chariot
swiftly enough,
I'll cure the rare sickness
of my sweetheart.

426. No need to go

Thalaivan to thalaivi:

My love,
with the war drums
booming their intent,
I'd have fought
the enemy king
to death.

But our king
carrying the winning spear
has decided against war.

427. Avoids fighting

Thalaivan to thalaivi:

My love,
Your large, flower-like eyes
provoke desire.
you won't allow me
to leave you
as the monsoon begins.

My warlike king, assuming
I won't come
to the battlefront
leaving you now,
has delayed fighting a war.

428. Let me look after you

Thalaivan to thalaivi:

Impeding the movement
of the chariot,
with a rainbow
bright on the sky,
the thundering black clouds
have brought downpours.

My king has freed me
from his esteemed task.
My duty is now
to look after you.

429. I won't go

Thalaivan to thalaivi:

My dark, dense-haired love,
the aggressive and untutored elephants
of our king's army
batter down the walls
of the enemy king
flying victory flags.

If your pallor persists,
I won't go.

430. Don't cry

Thalaivan to thalaivi:

On top of the tall hill
the short-trunked laburnum
blooms bright as a gold plate.

Daughter of the chieftain
of this forest country,
please don't cry.
I'll stop going.

44. Rain renews forest

In all the following ten poems the thozhi speaks consoling
words to thalaivi:

431. Flight of the peacocks

Friend, the path taken
by our lover is good.

On top of these colourful, huge hills
peacocks the colour of sapphire
fly about.

432. He is safe

Friend, the path taken
by our lover is good.

The laburnum shines
like beaten gold.
The warlike tribe
who inhabit the forest
are dressed like guests
attending a wedding.

433. Water everywhere

Friend, the path taken
by our lover is good.

The moist black clouds
bring down
monsoon rains
and there are forests too
all along the way.

434. Only deer

Friend, the path taken
by our lover is good.

After the rain
has pleasurably cooled the forest,
the stag and its mate
frolic with the fawn
in their wake.

435. Flowers everywhere

Friend, the path taken
by our lover is good.

The pale lily makes
the land pretty.
Golden laburnum
and wild jasmine
are found in plenty.

436. Flowers outdo each other

Friend, the path taken
by our friend is good.

Along with laburnum
with its clusters
of golden flowers,
the wild lime also is
in full bloom.

437. Jasmine laughs

Friend, the path taken
by our lover is good.

The falling hailstone
cools the land
and the white jasmine laughs.

438. A sight for the sore eye

Friend, the path taken
by our lover is good.

With the bushes brimming
with many-coloured flowers,
the forest has become
sweet and pleasant.

439. Friendly shepherds

Friend, the path taken
by our lover is good.

Along the way
there are dwellings
of shepherds
wearing *kurundam*
and ponds and lakes
brimful of water.

440. Rain renews

Friend, the path taken
by our lover is good.

The monsoon has brought
cool rains
and the bright-coloured
thondri and *thalavam*
keep rearing their heads.

45. In the military camp

441. Monsoon woes

Thalaivan to himself (after listening
to thalaivi's messenger):

Surprising are the charges
made by my sweet love.
Along with the thunder and rain
of these monsoon days,
her words have added
to my woes.

If only she knows
what I am going through here.

442. A feast on my return

The message from thalaivan to thalaivi:

If my furious king brings
this difficult business
to a closure,

my love who in chastity
is like *Arundhati*
residing in the dark skies
of the celestial world
and mother of my son
who wears tinklers
the size of a budding coconut
will host a feast on my return.

443. Shining like moon

The message from thalaivan to thalaivi:

My king who has
an honoured war drum
has captured the sky-high
defences of many a king.

If he brings
the war to an end,
without thinking about distance,
I'll mount my good chariot
and ride
till I see the brow of my love
shining like a young moon.

444. I'll get to see her

Thalaivan to himself:

The sharp tusks
of the war elephants
get blunted and their coverings broken
after assaults
on the long walls of the enemy.

If my king,
who wields a winning spear,
decides to return
to his own land
cooling hostilities,
I'll get to see
my plump-shouldered
young woman.

445. Animals are better off

Thalaivan to himself:

When I think of the season
in which young cows
follow the handsome bull,
my heart turns heavy.
O heart,
you've come
to this trying war camp
leaving my love
famed for her excellence, pining.

Worse, you've forced me too
to go there.

446. Decked with flowers

Thalaivan sees an image of thalaivi:

My dusky love,
after helping our king
in this difficult war business,
when I return
to our adorable and good country,

your hair,
smelling of jasmine,
will help us to explore
sweet pleasures.

447. I can make love

The bud of the red jasmine
grows in the mist
giving it the look
of a kingfisher's beak.
The winged bees
break this bud into blossom
humming a song.

To see
her bright-brow again
let my king be
freed of this war

448. Going haywire

The booming war drums
announce the morning.
My angry king makes
preparations for war.

Close to the soft pits,
the jasmine is in full bloom
as the monsoon has broken
with thundering rain.
Every time I think
of my long-haired love,
I lose sleep going haywire.

449. My mind is not here

The stone-strewn
hard earth shakes
as the chariot,
drawn by horses
which scorn the stable,
gets ready to move.

If my king frees me
from war duties,
I shall get to see
my bright-browed love.

450. Sighing like a furnace

Let my proud king put an end
to the hostilities and stop
the war drums sounding
on both sides
and think of returning
to his country.

To cure this sickness of love
which makes me sigh hot breaths,
let my eyes go to sleep
between the tender breasts
of my virtuous love.

46. The thalaivi at the onset of the monsoon

451. Poor timing

Thalaivi to herself:

It is the business of the king
to be with his unbeatable troops
to await the arrival of the enemy.

But he who left me helpless
when the monsoon
is breaking
should never avoid being
my guest riding his chariot.

452. Pale like the ridge gourd flower

Thalaivi to herself:

The roaring clouds
broke into rain
making the dry earth
come alive.

Whipping his enemies
and collecting tithes
from them
is what my lover likes most.

But the beauty
of my soft shoulders fades
becoming pale
like the ridge gourd flower.

453. No sign of his chariot

Thalaivi to thozhi:

Toads peep from pits
filled with water.
From high ground
sweet warblers sound.
Look, the monsoon has arrived.

Yet his chariot doesn't seem
to come my way.
And my big eyes
are dripping tears.

454. Drops of moonlight

Thalaivi to thozhi:

The tendrils of white jasmine
entwine the green stems
of the red jasmine.
Their sharp buds,
which look like
drops of moonlight,
wait for the monsoon
to open their petals.

My dusky beauty waits with love
the return of his chariot.

455. Thinner

Thalaivi to thozhi:

The monsoon clouds
begin thundering.
The kings reduce hostilities.
The beat of the angry
war drums subside.

My wide, soft shoulders are pitiable.
They become thinner,
their past beauty gone
and my bright jewels
have begun slipping.

456. Pale moon

Thalaivi to thozhi:

Friend, won't he
keep his promise?

Like the pale moon in daytime,
the white *paganrai* blooms
on top of the *ingai* shrub
lending beauty to it.

He left me
after breaking his promise
to be with me
before the unbearable
season of chill winds.

457. Miserable

Thalaivi to thozhi:

The falling mist makes
the herons miserable
which keep
sounding their distress.

In this season of togetherness
my lover cannot bear to leave me
nor can this fond heart
forget him and live.

458. A flower in the rain

Thalaivi to herself:

The flute-like fruits of laburnum,
growing in clusters,
have ripened much.
Its cool flowers,
battered by the thundering rain,
scatter and fall.

My lacklustre eyes
look like them
after my lover,
patron of minstrels, left me.

459. Give me a hug

Thalaivi to thozhi:

He is the chief of fertile farms
and lieutenant
to this aggressive king
whose army has broken
the battlements
of many an enemy.

To end the lovesickness
of my soft, arched shoulders,
will I be able to hug
his cool, sweet-smelling chest?

460. Pity me

Thalaivi to herself:

The furious king doesn't think
of leaving the war camp.
My lover
from the noisy hill country
sends no emissary.

Cold wind shakes
the thick-leaved banana tree
to its roots.
What will happen
to my poor self?

47. The thozhi consoles

Thozhi consoles thalaivi in the following ten poems.

461. He likes you

Friend, stop crying.
The fine rain falling
has made the wild jasmine
break into buds.
With the trees in the forest
scattering droplets,
the monsoon has begun.

Our lover,
staying in the camp
of the victorious king,
wouldn't like at all
to be away from you.

462. Make no mistake

Mistaking this untimely rain
for the arrival of monsoon
the ignorant laburnum
has begun to bloom
like strands of garland.

Woman,
what for is this sadness?
The lover who left us crossing
the forest of jasmine
is not hard-hearted.
He will not let
your beauty wither.

463. Choosing the right jewel

Friend,
he won't stay away
from you
without coming
to make your pretty hair
prettier still
with sweet flowers
which have begun
to bloom in the bush.

No doubt
he extends his stay for picking
the choicest of jewels
for your pretty sake
in the land of his beaten foe.

464. Cool season

The *karuvilai* blooms
like the eye
and the ridge gourd vine
on the bush
has flowers with a golden tint.

He who craved to hug
your sweet shoulders
will soon rush.
He won't forget this season.

465. He is coming

Your lover's chariot,
swift as a waterfall,
leaves behind the forest
lush after the rains.

His broad chest
which has various flowers
is yours to make love.
The king who loves wars
has cooled all hostilities.

466. He will return

You have all the sweetness
proper to a woman.
Your bright brow
fuels desire.
Your language is pure honey.

I am clear about one thing:
after doing his duty
as the king's envoy,
taking leave of the king
famed for his tuskers,
he'll return to you
on the appointed day.

467. Back to home

Friend, our king's elephants
are battle-scarred.
Our king himself is skilled
in winning combats.
Without further ado,
he is keen to get

his men back in their homes
more than we do.

So stop this pining.
It makes your
well-fitting jewels fall down.

468. Feast to you

The striped frogs croak,
the toads take up the chorus.
The monsoon has broken
with a bang.

To be a feast to your soft shoulders
and slender arms,
he'll arrive today
with the bells
in his long chariot clanging.

469. Let's watch the rain

The red-feathered quail
steals the green millet
in the forests of our lover.
To restore him to us
the clouds swirl from right to left
and bring down rain.
The vast sky resonates
with peals of thunder.

My friend,
you have eyes like flowers.
Come, let's watch.

470. A beautiful reminder

Bejewelled friend,
the chill wind blows
cooling the vast land
and brings in its wake
unbearable fog.

Even if this season
does not make
your lover think of you,
your dusky beauty
will surely remind.

48. The bard as messenger

471. Be considerate

Thozhi to bard:

Bard, my friend's bright bangles
have loosened.
She's grown thinner.
Her kohled eyes,
pretty like the lily,
have become bleary
in the sweeping cold wave.

Her lover,
caught in the heat of war,
has forgotten all about her.
You're coming as his messenger
because you know
nothing about it.
How very considerate he is!

472. Promises ignored

Thozhi to bard:

Bard, you're a virtuoso
in playing the harp.
The season appointed
by your chief
for his return
has arrived and taken root.

Even if he doesn't sense it
for our sake,
I'm pained
at his utter disregard
for the promises he made.

473. An expert liar

Thalaivi to bard:

We know your skill
in playing the harp.

If you wish to go after your chief
whose virtues
are valorized by many
and who has caused us
much suffering,
at least don't forget us
as he did.

474. The faithful bard

Thalaivi to bard:

The chief has shattered
the defences of his enemies
with his hardened troops.
His galloping horses have drawn
his long chariot leaving long tracks.

Yet the bard says
he'll bring him back
to make my spotless
brow bright again.
How wise he is!

475. Unlike the chief

Thalaivi to thozhi:

My shoulders have shrunk
loosening my armlets.
My lustreless eyes,
which had the look
of a tender mango,
incite the pity of this bard
skilled in playing the little harp.

Unlike the chief,
whom I love a lot
but who left me to suffer,
this bard is very tender.

476. No love for me

Thalaivi to bard:

Bard, you've no love for me.
Lightning and thunder
flash in the sky which opens up.
Jasmine begins to bloom
on green stems
in seasons such as this.
The cowherds make
garlands of leaves
and weave these flowers
into them.

Are such loveless evenings
there in the country
he is visiting?

477. Stay with her

Thalaivan to bard:

Bard, her large eyes
used to look like cool flowers.
They must now be riddled
with lovesickness.
Agonizing thoughts
must be passing through
her grief-stricken mind.

If you stay with her awhile
as relief to her helpless heart,
you'll see my chariot soon.

478. Tell me her exact words

Thalaivan to bard:

Bard, you're good at playing
the music of mullai.

Thinking that I am delaying
my return on purpose,
she tells about my cruelty
with a brow
that has lost all its shine
and thinks contrarian thoughts.

Tell me what she said,
the frail woman
whom I love a lot.

479. Let me hear her through you

Thalaivan to bard:

Speak to me bard.
I have crossed countries
and the harsh, chill wind mocks
at my loneliness every day.

Speak to me
the sweet words of the woman
whose eyes are pretty
like flowers with dew drops.

480. I resign

Bard to thalaivan:

The woman
who loves you so much
cries alone at home
and if you're unmoved
even after listening
to the suffering
of her kohled, wet eyes,
I'm not a bard to you
and you're no longer my chief.

49. Drive the chariot faster

Thalaivan urges his charioteer to drive faster in the following
ten poems:

481. Sad state

Charioteer,
her full shoulders
have the look
of a curved moon
and her mound is beautifully lined.
Her jewels are red in colour.

To rid my
sad state of sickness,
urge your horses
swift as birds
with a touch of your whip
with a thorn.

482. Longer than an age

Charioteer, to be a grand feast
to the young woman
who chooses her jewels well,
drive faster.

Even if I stay for a day
with the king
whose army carries
bright spears
which annihilate enemies,
it will appear
longer than an age.

483. Duty done

Charioteer,
the paths are beautiful
with fallen flowers.
The king has freed me
as the duty is done.

The horses are moving
at a fast clip.
To restore the beauty
of my sweet-browed woman,
drive the chariot still faster.

484. Make your name known

Charioteer, the summer left
after the monsoon broke.
The forest wears a beautiful look.
I have kept
my bejewelled woman
out of my mind
for quite a long while.

Drive your chariot faster still,
to make its name widely known.

485. Let me end her agony

Charioteer,
to relieve the unbearable agony
she is going through,
and make love
to restore the health
of her ample shoulders,

drive the chariot faster
through the flower-filled woods
in which timid deer gambol.

486. Teasing evenings

Charioteer,
the evenings are hurtful
as the unceasing thoughts
of a rare affliction
trouble the lovers.
Let her not feel it.

We loved each other every day,
yet my love for her
has not lessened.
Holding the reins skilfully,
urge your horses
swift as birds
to make the chariot run faster.

487. A time to love

This is the time
when parted lovers
think of each other.

To delight my love
who wears fitting armlets,
my sensible charioteer,
drive faster.

488. She longs for me

The sky has opened up
with thunder and lightning.
This is the time when my love,
known for her winning ways,
longs for me.

Yoking excellent horses
with broad mane,
drive faster to rid her of sorrow.

489. Run faster

Swarms of winged bees
buzz on jasmine
that blooms in evenings
in the wooded forest.

To please the suffering heart
of my ladylove,
urge your sturdy horses
pulling the long chariot
to run faster
tugging at the reins
made of twisted rope.

490. Tinkle bells

This monsoon has come
to unite me
with my sweet-tongued love.
To end the terrible suffering
of one who chooses
her armlets well,

drive your long chariot faster still,
to the tinkling of its bells.

50. The thalaivan's return after assignment

491. The magnet

Thalaivan to thalaivi:

Sweet love, the monsoon clouds
gather and roar
troubling me without a break.
With a disgruntled mind
occupied by unhinging thoughts
I hurried to you
to return your beauty.

492. Everything reminds you

Thalaivan to thalaivi:

The peacock danced just like you.
Like your sweet brow
the jasmine bloomed,
the deer timidly looked about
just as you do.

My pretty-browed woman,
I thought only of you
as I hurried
faster than the monsoon clouds.

493. Start of the monsoon

Thalaivan to thalaivi:

My love,
your hand looks beautiful
with all these bangles.

When I was returning
thinking about you,
the bulls replied
to the roar of the thunder.

The handsome stag,
with its mate and fawn, frolicked.
They signalled the start
of the monsoon.

494. Let your sorrow end

Thalaivan to thalaivi:

While the winged bees
feast on honey,
the toads begin to peep.
In the cool forest
the fragrance of jasmine
is everywhere.
It is a pleasurable season.

I've returned at the appointed time.
Let your sorrow end.

495. Red earth and blooming flowers

Thalaivan to thalaivi:

My love,
your teeth are sharp as thorns.

When I walked with a heavy heart
thinking about you,
and how your plaited hair
will look better
if flowers are worn,

a score of flowers blooming
on the red earth
drove away my loneliness
making the forest
sweet indeed.

496. Let your hair wear flowers again

Thozhi to thalaivi:

My large, limpid-eyed friend,
the deer look
for refuge in the bushes.
The millet fills
its husk with milk.
The tall mountains
look lonely.
The thundering black clouds
bring down sharp showers.

Your lover who left you
has come back
to be your companion.
Let your long hair
begin to love flowers again.

497. He returned with the monsoon

Thozhi to thalaivi:

My beautiful friend,
you have a noble nature.
Our chief who left us
out of his love for war
has returned thinking about you.

And the monsoon has returned
along with him.
Clusters of laburnum bloom
like a garland
and white ants swarm
out of tall, red termite hills
and the animals,
made miserable by the chill wind,
refuse food.

498. Demobbed

Thozhi to thalaivi:

The king who led
an army of tuskers
has freed our chief of the hills
from war duties.
He has now returned
in his swift-moving long chariot.

With his return,
your shoulders have regained
their beauty.
Bangles stay in their place.
The long-lined large eyes
have got back their
sparkle and allure.

499. He kept his appointment

Thozhi to thalaivi:

My friend, your speech is sweet.
Varieties of jasmine bloom
and bring forth their buds.
'If she sees the forest

in all its beauty
at break of monsoon,
she'll be very sad.'

Thinking so,
our lover has returned
without lengthening his stay
in the battlefront
to restore your beauty.

500. Back in its lair

Thozhi to thalaivan:

Her eyes, lovesick, drooping
like the flowers of laburnum,
became like a lily
in the large pond
close to the hills.

They got back
their past beauty
when the chief,
victor of many a battle,
returned from the vast war camp
like a strong tiger.

NOTES

V. Mullai
Peyanar

41. The foster mother's report

Sent to find out how matters stand at the thalaivi's household, the foster mother brings such news of domestic bliss as to gladden the heart of any mother. She paints an idyllic picture of contentment and love among thalaivan and thalaivi and their infant son. These are also the poems that celebrate the *karpu neri*, life after marriage in contrast to the earlier *kalavu neri*, love before marriage. These ten poems are unparalleled for the portraits of conjugal love they present.

401. Ancient Tamils placed familial love above everything else.
402. The *Kural* (66) says that those who have never heard of their kids' baby talk alone will praise the music of instruments.
403. The birth of paternal love, no less.
404. The thalaivan and thalaivi now have someone else to focus on—their own baby.
405. The thalaivi, who had till then been a daughter, is now elevated to the status of the mother who lights up the household. The bride is expected to light the lamp on her arrival even today. *Mullai* means forest as well as the jasmine that grows there. It is in italics only when it refers to the flower.
406. Even a male baby is marked with kohl and a small black dot placed on its cheek to ward off the evil eye.

407. The harmony of the bard's music blends with domestic harmony.
408. Every *tinai* had its own particular music just as it had its own predominant mood, season, landscape and flower.
410. It is a 'defining' moment of domestic bliss.

42. The thalaivan returns before the monsoon

When the thalaivan returns before the monsoon, it not only means he keeps his word to her but also shows the consideration he has for her as this season could be quite cruel to the lonely lover.

411. '*Pudu punal adal*' or swimming in the fresh floods is customary for the newly-wedded.
412. The summer drains the colour of the landscape making it desert-like. The monsoon returns it.
413. This reverse simile, unlike the ironic simile, intensifies the effect.
414. The birds, beasts and plants are joyful.
415. Not a seduction piece like Marvell's "Coy Mistress" but the satisfaction of mutual love after a tense separation.
416. Observe the oneness of man with his environs.
417. 'The fields are full of ploughshares' is a dense image. As George Hart says, 'In general, the comparison of a woman to a field is made to suggest that the woman is a sexual object; the act of union is compared to the sowing of the field with seed.'(163)
418. The bliss felt by the thalaivan is not of this world.
419. A lesson is to be drawn from the animals that know 'no separation.'
420. The forest in bloom will make her happier.

43. The miscellany

423 & 424. Separation, a theme proper to palai, occurs in mullai. Scholars designate this intrusion as '*tinai*

mayakkam' or confusion of moods which is not so much an error as an overlapping.

426. Not fighting a battle during the monsoon is an unwritten code of war usually honoured by both armies.

427. The king assumes that the heart of thalaivan, a valuable lieutenant, will be with his wife.

428. The movement of the chariot was bogged down by the monsoon slush.

44. The rain renews the forest

431-440. In a landscape quiet as this, nothing untoward will happen to thalaivan, seems to be the thozhi's message. *Konrai* is laburnum, *neidal*, pale water lily; *pidavam* is wild jasmine, *thondri*, malabar glory lily or *kantal* and *thalavam* refers to the wild pink jasmine.

45. In the military camp

Separated from thalaivi because of the war business and tormented by the arrival of the monsoon, the thalaivan is homesick and lovesick.

441. The thalaivi's message berates the thalaivan for not keeping his promise to return before the monsoon.

442. *Arundhati* is the wife of *Vasishta* who is one of the seven stars known as '*Sapta Rishi*' or Ursa Major. She has come to symbolize wifely devotion and chastity.

443. The king's success depends on sensing the pulse of his men. He must not only know how to initiate a war but also how to bring it to an end. Fighting a war during monsoon is bad strategy.

444. Winning the war may spur the king on to fighting many more battles.

445. There is a dichotomy between the thalaivan and his heart.

447. The comparison of the long, slender bud of the red jasmine with the red beak of the kingfisher is a happy image.
448. The appearance of the soft jasmine close to aggressive war images corresponds to the lovelorn heart of the thalaivan.

46. The monsoon has come but not the thalaivan

454. The jasmine waiting for the monsoon to open its petals and the thalaivi waiting for the thalaivan are analogous.
456. *Paganrai* is Indian jalap flower and *ingai* refers to the touch-me-not.

47. The thozhi consoles

462. The thozhi seems to be telling the thalaivi not to make the same mistake that the laburnum made, i.e. mistaking the showers for the arrival of the monsoon.
463. The defeated king and his country were subjected to many humiliations. The men were asked to eat grass, their royal avenues were ploughed and their fertile farms ransacked. Any wealth that he had belonged to the conquering king.
464. *Karuvilai* is *sanguppu* in lay Tamil. It grows in a small-sized bush.
465. The thozhi as the bearer of good tidings.

48. The bard as messenger

477. The bard's arrival foretells the arrival of the chief.
478. Even the bitter words of thalaivi imply her love for him.
479. The words of his love, even if spoken by the bard, are music to the ears of the thalaivan.
480. The bard is carrying out his duty as the unifier of lovers by speaking out in the strongest terms.

49. Drive the chariot faster

Ten poems which convey the urgency of the lover to be back with his lady.

481. Such sexual explicitness to the charioteer may sound strange but frankness in voicing their sexual urges is characteristic of Sangam poetry.
482. The thalaivan often carried out duties as the envoy of his king.
483. There is no more reason to hold the thalaivan back.
486. The thalaivan wishes that the chariot must become airborne.
489. Jasmine is a flower beloved of lovers for its rather giddy fragrance.

50. The thalaivan's return after the assignment

492. The peacock, the jasmine and the deer only intensify the thalaivan's longing for the thalaivi as they only succeed in reminding him of her.
495. Sounds very similar to the daffodils surprising and pleasing Wordsworth. Comparing the teeth of thalaivi to sharp thorns, jasmine buds and new sprouts is common in classical Tamil literature.
496. Perhaps the thalaivi stopped wearing flowers on her hair on account of her sorrow.
497. Though the monsoon brought its own privations to the animal world, the humans normally rejoiced at its arrival.
498. The forest in full bloom is pleasing to the thalaivi only in the company of thalaivan.
500. The return of thalaivan signals the return of thalaivi's beauty too.

SELECT
BIBLIOGRAPHY

Hart, George. *The Poems of Ancient Tamil: Their Milieu and Their Sanskrit Counterparts*. New Delhi, OUP, 1999.

Iraiyanar Akaporrul with commentary by Nakkirar. Tirunelveli: The South India Saiva Sithantha Works, 1953. Rep. 1964.

Konar, A. Karmegha, et al. *Ainkurunutru Chorpozhivugal*. Tirunelveli: Saiva Sithantha Kazhakam, 1965.

Manickam V. Sp. *The Tamil Concept of Love in Ahattinai*. Tirunelveli: Saiva Sithantha Works, 1962.

Ramanujan A. K. Trans. *Poems of Love and War: From the Eight Anthologies and the Ten Long Poems of Classical Tamil*. Delhi: OUP, 1985.

Selby, Martha Ann. *Tamil Love Poetry: The Five Hundred Short Poems of the Ainkurunuru*. New York: Columbia University Press, 2011.

Somasundaranar. P.V. *Ainkurunuru with Commentary*. Tirunelveli: Saiva Sithanth Works, 1979.

Thangappa, M. L. Trans. *Love Stands Alone: Selections from Tamil Sangam Poetry*. New Delhi. Penguin-Viking, 2010.

Varadarajan M. *The Treatment of Nature in Sangam Literature*. Tirunelveli: South India Saiva Siddhantha. 1969.

Zvelebil, Kamil V. *Literary Conventions in Akam Poetry*. Madras: Institute of Asian Studies, 1986.

—.*Companion Studies to the History of Tamil Literature*. Leiden: E.J. Brill.1992.

INDEX